Managing CAD/CAM

Managing CAD/CAM

Implementation, Organization, and Integration

John Stark

McGraw-Hill Book Company

New York St. Louis San Francisco Auckland
Bogotá Hamburg London Madrid Mexico
Milan Montreal New Delhi Panama
Paris São Paulo Singapore
Sydney Tokyo Toronto

MANAGING CAD/CAM
INTERNATIONAL EDITION

1 2 3 4 5 6 7 8 9 0 BJE PMP 8 9 4 3 2 1 0 9

The editors for this book were Betty Sun and Rita T. Margolies.
The designer was Naomi Auerbach.
The production supervisor was Diane Walber.
It was set in Century Schoolbook.
It was composed by the McGraw-Hill Book Company Professional & Reference Division composition unit.

Library of Congress Cataloging-in-Publication Data

Stark, John, date
Managing CAD/CAM.
Includes index.
1. CAD/CAM systems–Management. 2. CAD/CAM systems–Planning. I. Title.
TS155.6.S729 1988 670'.28'5 88-8903
ISBN 0-07-060876-8

When ordering this title use ISBN 0-07-100913-2

Printed in Singapore

For Alicja

and

for Jasna,
"une fille formidable"

Contents

Preface

Since the early 1960s, when the first steps toward CAD/CAM were taken, many books have been written about the subject. Why then has another one been written, and even more important, why should busy engineers read it?

Most of the earlier books tended to describe mainly the components and potential benefits of CAD/CAM without addressing its use and management. Typically, they describe how computers, graphics screens, plotters, and other CAD/CAM equipment function and give an overview of some CAD/CAM application areas, such as drafting, NC programming, and stress analysis. They may also describe some CAD/CAM systems that are on the market and the types of geometric modelers that exist.

The subject of this book, though, is the use of CAD/CAM within industry. Although the title of the book indicates that it is essential reading for industry's CAD/CAM managers, it will also be of interest to other managers of industrial companies and to those who support and use CAD/CAM systems. Perhaps it may even, by describing some of the problems associated with use of CAD/CAM, be of use to developers of CAD/CAM systems.

CAD/CAM is a technique that has the potential to greatly improve the quality, flow, and use of engineering information within a company. Most of the previously published books have assumed that this potential would automatically be translated into productivity gains—reductions in costs and in time cycles, and an improvement in quality. However, experience shows that this process is by no means automatic, and one of the major objectives of this book is to describe some of the activities that must be undertaken if the dream is to become reality and real benefits are to result from the use of CAD/CAM.

The book is primarily addressed to the CAD/CAM manager because, from the CAD/CAM point of view, this is the person in the company who holds the key to success. The reason for the importance of this role and the responsibilities attached to it are outlined at the beginning of the book.

CAD/CAM should not be an "island of automation" independent of the other activities of the company. The book looks at some of the ways in which, right from the start, CAD/CAM must be managed so that it becomes a part of the overall engineering operations of the company. Although it must fit into the overall structure, it has, nevertheless, some rather specific characteristics that make it very different from the other parts. The organization of CAD/CAM activities needs to reflect these differences. Similarly, a new approach is needed by management to ensure that people contribute as fully as possible to the successful development of the CAD/CAM resource.

The book starts off by explaining how to develop an environment in which CAD/CAM can be used successfully and goes on to show how to achieve and maintain productive use. Particular attention is paid to training, data management, and implementation and use of effective procedures. Finally, the longer term is addressed. In a company that is using CAD/CAM successfully, the overall resources committed to CAD/CAM will increase, and the integration of CAD/CAM with other activities in the company will continue. The last chapter of the book describes the way in which this process can be managed and how the resources committed to CAD/CAM can be used in the most effective way.

John Stark

Acknowledgments

I would like to thank the following people in the Coopers & Lybrand organization for major contributions to the preparation of this book:

Denis Hall (C&L Toronto, Canada) Chapter 2

Guy Marguerat (STH Egg, Switzerland) Chapter 6

Ben Anthony (C&L Uxbridge, England) Chapter 9

Roger Tempest (C&L Uxbridge, England) Chapter 11

The assistance of the following is also acknowledged. Mireille Tempez (C&L Paris, France), John Levis (C&L Manchester, England), Chris Bennett (C&L Geneva, Switzerland), and Graham Browne (C&L Cambridge, England).

Thanks are also due to the following for their help at various times during preparation of the book. J. Beale (C&L San José, California); R. Bleasdale (C&L Uxbridge, England); L. Hales (Systecon Atlanta, Georgia); W. L. Howard (C&L Washington, D.C.); D. Macdonald (C&L Reading, England); K. Müller (STH Basel, Switzerland); M. Neuve Eglise (C&L Paris, France); L. Reeve (C&L San Francisco, California).

Finally thanks are due to Alice Ibrahim for word processing.

Chapter 1

An Introduction to CAD/CAM and the CAD/CAM Manager's Role

1.1 Introduction

Computer-aided design engineering and computer-aided manufacturing engineering (CAD/CAM) will be a key component of successful engineering practice in the 1990s. Although the basic hardware of CAD/CAM, such as the computer, numerical control, and the graphics screen, has been available since the 1960s, suitable software (particularly in the fields of geometric modeling and engineering data management) has not. Until the introduction of microcomputer-based CAD/CAM systems in the mid-1980s, CAD/CAM appeared too expensive to the vast majority of engineering companies. People take time to adjust to new technologies and to take full advantage of them. It also takes time to build up experience in applying new technologies to specific areas. The 1960s, 1970s, and 1980s can be seen, on one hand, as decades in which CAD/CAM matured and became an immensely powerful technique and, on the other hand, as decades in which people learned how to make the best use of CAD/CAM. In the 1990s these two elements will come together, and it will be very difficult for an engineering company to survive unless it makes effective use of CAD/CAM.

CAD/CAM will not succeed in a company unless it receives widespread support. Without the support of top management, it will not contribute usefully to meeting the company's strategic objectives. Without the support of middle management, it will not be widely introduced and used in engineering and other areas of the company. Without the support of engineering personnel it will clearly fail.

Experience shows that the successful introduction and use of

CAD/CAM also depends, to a very large extent, on the CAD/CAM manager. The CAD/CAM manager is the major link between the CAD/CAM policy decisions of top management and the users of CAD/CAM. The role of the CAD/CAM manager will be described in more detail later. Briefly, it includes involvement in defining policy, administering everyday affairs, ensuring that objectives are met, coordinating activities, leading and motivating people, and ensuring that an effective organization is in place.

One of the problems facing the CAD/CAM manager is that different people, inside and outside the company, will have different views of CAD/CAM. The fact that these views are different does not necessarily mean that they are incorrect or incompatible. As an analogy, the front, side, top, and rear views of a car are different but not incorrect or incompatible. In the same way that the different views of a car are just different representations of the same thing (the car), the different views that people have of CAD/CAM should just be different representations of the overall company CAD/CAM philosophy.

In many companies, however, people have had irreconcilably different views of CAD/CAM. The result generally has been confusion, lost time, and wasted investment. To avoid this situation, the CAD/CAM manager needs to make sure that the overall company CAD/CAM philosophy is publicized, understood, and accepted.

In the rest of this chapter, examples are given of some different points of view. Some are those of people outside the company (those of the CAD/CAM vendor, the management consultant, the client). The others are all typical views of people within the company.

1.2 CAD/CAM—The Vendor's View

The first applications of CAD/CAM took place in the early 1960s. Since then the use of CAD/CAM has become widespread, and it is now used in a wide range of industries, such as aerospace, automobile, offshore engineering, machine, machine-tool, domestic appliance, footwear, clothing, engineering, electronics, shipbuilding, plant engineering, scientific instrument, and die and mold-making.

CAD (computer-aided design engineering) has an even wider range of use. It can be found in drafting departments and design offices of all sorts, public organizations, architects' offices, and government and design consultancies and bureaus.

CAD/CAM is used by companies of all sizes. It is used by some of the largest companies in the world, such as General Motors, and also by some of the smallest, for example, companies with less than

20 employees. CAD/CAM is in use in more than 60 countries. The number of CAD/CAM workstations installed worldwide is about half a million. The number of users per workstation is generally between 2:1 and 3:1, so there are more than a million users of CAD/CAM screens worldwide. The total spent on CAD/CAM systems up to 1987 exceeds $20 billion. In 1988 about $3.5 billion will be spent on CAD/CAM systems.

CAD/CAM is used in many different areas of the overall design, engineering, and manufacturing process. These areas include marketing, proposal preparation, styling, conceptual design, structural analysis, kinematic analysis, simulation, engineering design, engineering tests, detailed design, schematic and wiring layout design, drafting, parts list and technical documentation preparation, plant layout, process planning, tool and fixture design, numerical control (NC) machine-tool programming, robot programming, NC quality control machine programming, programmable logic controller (PLC) programming, and materials-handling simulation. It is used in preparing for a variety of manufacturing processes, including the forming of metals, plastics, rubber, leather, composites, glass, and ceramics, and the cutting of metals, fabrics, leather, and composites. It is also used in preparing for paint spraying, composite laying, parts assembly, and deburring.

The basic hardware components of CAD/CAM include the computer, the graphics screen, the tablet, the menu, the engineering workstation, and the plotter. The major components of the software include the graphics software (to control the picture on the screen), the computer's operating system (to control the actions of the computer and the input and output of data to data storage devices and other peripheral equipment), the part-modeling software (to allow the user to build up a representation, called the *model*, of the part in the computer), and the data management software (to allow the user to store and retrieve information).

There are many benefits that can arise from use of CAD/CAM. They include simplified updating of designs, a reduction in the number of prototypes needed, more reliable production of parts lists, a reduction in NC machine-tool programming time, an increase in the use of standard parts, a reduction in cycle times, a reduction in costs, and an increase in quality.

CAD/CAM is seen to be one of the building blocks of the "factory of the future," computer integrated manufacturing (CIM), or of the "paperless factory." Clearly, any engineering company without CAD/CAM should purchase a system as soon as possible, and those companies that already have CAD/CAM should expand their systems.

1.3 CAD/CAM—The Client's View

Our company is based in Pittsburgh. We used to buy special components from three companies, one in Detroit, one in Columbus, Ohio, and the other in Buffalo, New York. A few years back, the Detroit company, which also works a lot with the automobile manufacturers, was told by one of its big clients that it was time to get into CAD/CAM. Soon after, they started quoting much shorter lead times. The people in Buffalo found out about this, and about a year later they bought a CAD/CAM system and started quoting shorter lead times too. The people in Columbus thought that it was too early to get into CAD/CAM. We don't know what they're doing now since they no longer work with us. As time has gone on, the people in Buffalo have managed to continuously decrease costs and lead times. They tell us that it's mainly due to their use of CAD/CAM. That's funny really because the people in Detroit have also got CAD/CAM, but after that one-time reduction in lead times, they didn't offer us any real improvements at all. We think that there was something wrong with the way they managed CAD/CAM, but we don't really know. It doesn't really matter as we don't work with them any more.

1.4 CAD/CAM—The Management Consultant's View

Many companies bought CAD/CAM systems because they believed that they would, as a consequence, achieve productivity gains of 50:1 to 5:1 (depending on industry sector and application area). In practice, many of them have found it extremely difficult to achieve any productivity gain at all. Others tell of a drop in productivity for 3 years before eventually seeing gains in the fourth year.

It appears that many companies failed to see CAD/CAM as a strategic tool for successful engineering. Instead, they saw it as a way to increase the speed of producing drawings. This invariably meant that the overall productivity increase was very small. Even among those companies that recognized the strategic nature of CAD/CAM, there seems to have been a failure to understand that successful use of CAD/CAM does not automatically follow from purchase of a system. It is a technique that is not easy to implement, and a lot of effort has to be put into its management and organization. Another strange thing is that top managers very rarely know whether CAD/CAM is really being used effectively in their companies. Often when they are asked whether their implementation of CAD/CAM has met the objectives, they find it difficult to reply. Sometimes, perhaps, there were no objectives set, and often it seems that no one has tried to find out what real progress has been made. In that case, experienced consultants can generally help a company increase the benefits it gets from CAD/CAM.

1.5 CAD/CAM—The "Engineering Information" View

The fundamental objective of the introduction of CAD/CAM by a company is to improve the use, flow, and quality of engineering information. The introduction of CAD/CAM should be an action resulting from the implementation of the manufacturing and information strategies of the company. Clearly, these strategies should be part of the overall company strategy. If not, there is only a small chance that it will succeed in helping the company attain its objectives.

Most of the benefits that are supposed to result from the introduction of CAD/CAM can be attained by the vast majority of companies. Once all the information describing a part has been defined and stored in an accessible way using the CAD/CAM system, that information does not have to be re-created, but can be reused. Creation of information takes time and costs money. Consequently, reducing the need to re-create information saves time and money. Before the introduction of CAD/CAM, many companies would re-create information on the same part between 5 and 10 times (e.g., in design, analysis, drafting, part-programming, and process planning). At each step, there was the risk that an error would be introduced so that eventually the part that was manufactured was not exactly the same as the part that had been designed to meet customer requirements. With CAD/CAM, the information only needs to be created once; thus the risk of introducing transcription errors is removed.

The information stored in the CAD/CAM system can be of much higher quality and precision than that previously available. If necessary a complex part can be designed to an accuracy of 10 microns, and the corresponding part can then be machined. With manual methods the time for this process would have been measured in weeks or months, with CAD/CAM it becomes a matter of days. CAD/CAM can therefore help a company improve its services to customers and simultaneously beat off the competition.

There is no doubt that CAD/CAM is a very powerful tool and can produce some amazing results. So why do so many companies fail to achieve such results? The problem does not lie with the CAD/CAM technology itself, but in the way in which it is managed by the company, and in the way in which the company is organized.

The importance of correctly managing the introduction and use of CAD/CAM is often underestimated. It should not be forgotten that the fundamental objective of the introduction of CAD/CAM is to improve the use, flow, and quality of engineering information. Information is an important company asset, and consequently the technologies, such as CAD/CAM, that "handle" information are of strategic importance. If top management fails to understand the importance of CAD/CAM, it is unlikely that sufficient resources will be assigned to it.

There is, therefore, an initial requirement that top management understand the potential of CAD/CAM and the need to place it in the context of the overall manufacturing and information strategies of the company. Objectives need to be set for the use of CAD/CAM and then communicated to all those making decisions involving CAD/CAM. Without these objectives, people in different parts of the company will develop their own "islands" or "empires" of CAD/CAM, and the results obtained may be minor compared to those expected. Only top management can set the objectives, and only top management can decide how much will be invested in CAD/CAM, how it will be financed, how the investment will be recovered from use of CAD/CAM, and what return on investment is required.

Top management must also be aware that successful use of CAD/CAM is rarely achieved without introducing changes in organizational structure and in people's work content. Again, this results from the objective to improve the use, flow, and quality of engineering information. The need to introduce changes implies that pre-CAD/CAM organizational structures and tasks are not particularly effective from the viewpoint of engineering information. This is hardly surprising since most organizations are based on principles of splitting the overall requirements of production into a multitude of virtually independent subtasks that can be carried out by human beings of below-average intelligence. Depending on the size of the company, there will be a plethora of divisions, departments, groups, sectors, etc., with a large quantity of managers, supervisors, and group leaders trying to coordinate their subordinates' actions. A typical company may have a purchasing department, an engineering department, a production department, and a sales department which should all use the engineering information concerning a product. The act of dividing the company into separate "manageable" departments creates artificial barriers to the flow of information. Thus the engineering department may well see its final product as a drawing of the product that is given to the production department (and then forgotten about). The production department (which probably never sees the customer) believes that its job is to produce whatever is on the drawing received from the engineering department—within the bounds of common sense, available funds, their own knowledge, and various other factors. They may well decide to interpret the drawing to best suit themselves, and hence produce something that the customer did not ask for. Although this sounds absurd, it is relatively commonplace.

It would appear that design and manufacturing engineers should jointly define all the engineering information concerning a product in conjunction with other interested parties (e.g., marketing). This is quite possible with CAD/CAM technology. However, it is often very difficult because traditional organizational structures do not encourage people to cross departmental barriers. Similarly, the power of the CAD/CAM technology will sometimes allow a person in one department to do not only his or her own job but also that of someone in another department.

The power of CAD/CAM technology can also increase the capabilities and degree of responsibility of individuals in the organization. The organization, which was set up on the assumption that most individuals had to be supervised by several layers of management, finds itself faced with intelligent and capable individuals frustrated by the confines of the traditional organization and unwilling to support the load of unnecessary administrative managers. At the same time, of course, the managers become very worried about their own future in the company, since their traditional skills no longer appear to be needed.

Pressure is put on the organization from two sides: first from the requirement to use engineering information more effectively, and second from the aspirations of individuals to carry out tasks with a content that is interesting and enriching, rather than the uninteresting tasks that result from an arbitrary division that took place in the past.

There are so many changes occurring in the manufacturing industry as a result of new applications of technology that it will be increasingly difficult for an individual to keep up with them. Part of the solution lies in increasing the amount of training that companies give their employees. In the 1990s, many companies will be spending 5 to 10 percent of total personnel costs on employee training and education. Once again, this will create an organizational problem. The company will not want to lose its highly trained workers, but the typical traditional organization is often incapable of holding on to such staff because there is no way for them to move "upward" (in position, in salary, or in peer recognition) within such a structure. To maintain talented staff, organizations will have to change and offer higher levels of job interest and broader responsibilities.

Effective use of engineering information leads to challenges in management, in organization, and in the attitudes of the company and its employees. These challenges must be met, because competitors will meet them. The company that prefers to do nothing will go to the wall.

1.6 CAD/CAM—The "Integrated Business" View

Traditional manufacturing companies are characterized by rigid departmental barriers separating functional areas. This has led to departments such as engineering, manufacturing, finance, personnel, and marketing behaving as independent fiefdoms. Contacts between departments are reduced to the minimum possible, and occur through bureaucratic channels. Within each department, managers do almost as they please, independently implementing whatever sort of computer systems appear to meet their short-sighted and blinkered aims. In such an environment, employees have little feeling of belonging to the company, still less of serving customers. Instead, they feel as if they belong to a department engaged in a battle for survival against the other departments of the company.

CIM is one expression of a feeling that perhaps manufacturing companies could be run better. The concept that is believed to be of assistance is "integration." The aim is for the company to become an integrated manufacturing company. Included among the beliefs of the integrated manufacturing company are that all employees are working for one and the same company, and that all employees are working toward the common objective of a quality product for the customer. With people and processes planned together and working together, the integrated manufacturing company will outperform the traditional manufacturing company.

In an integrated manufacturing company, people work together, they have a good understanding of their roles and the company's aims, they can ask each other questions, and they can share resources. As an example, consider the following everyday requirements of people in a manufacturing company.

Marketing is preparing a proposal and needs some drawings of existing parts from engineering.

Sales has a potential client who needs a "special" produced in less than 3 months. Can production schedule this?

Before designing a new part, engineering wants to check with stores to see which similar parts are available.

For another product, engineering wants to know the estimated cost of two alternative designs. They need to talk to purchasing.

Someone on the shop floor has found a way to reduce by 50 percent the production time of a part that is being made in batches of 50. Only three batches have been made so far. They need to talk to engineering.

The client for that batch of 50 has just called sales to request modifications to the geometry of two parts in the batch. Will engineering be able to produce new NC machining and quality control programs in time?

In the traditional manufacturing company, the answer to these questions would be to put up the departmental barriers and tell "them" (i.e., the client) to come back in a month.

In the integrated manufacturing company, solutions will be found as quickly as possible—in a few minutes, or a few hours. This will only be possible if the right information is available and can be communicated to whoever needs it. Information is seen to be an important corporate asset and is used accordingly. What will be the view of CAD/CAM in such a company?

One of the first objectives of such a company will be to develop an integrated manufacturing strategy and a corresponding plan. This will required the identification of the information needs of people throughout the company. It will be seen that engineers require information from many parts of the company, and that people in many areas require information from engineering.

The role of the CAD/CAM system will be to serve as a tool for engineers to build up and store product information, to supply this information to other parts of the company, and to allow engineers to access information from other parts of the company.

1.7 CAD/CAM—The Design Manager's View

Much has been written on the topics of design, design engineering, and what constitutes good design. There can only be one answer to "What constitutes good design"? That is, a successful product is the outcome of good design. However, "successful product" must be qualified. Is a product successful because it sells in volume in a consumer market; or is it successful if it meets the rigorous specification laid down by, let us say, a defense contractor; or is the real measure of success that it contributes toward the profitability of the company that has designed and manufactured it? It is, of course, all of these, but with a different emphasis depending on the type of business that the company is in.

Figure 1.1 shows the major relationships between design parameters but omits two important and interrelated issues in design engineering management: namely, an infinite amount of time to design and develop a product is never available, and specifications rarely remain frozen.

Market forces demand reduced lead times, thus increasing the complexity of the product design process. A major problem for all design

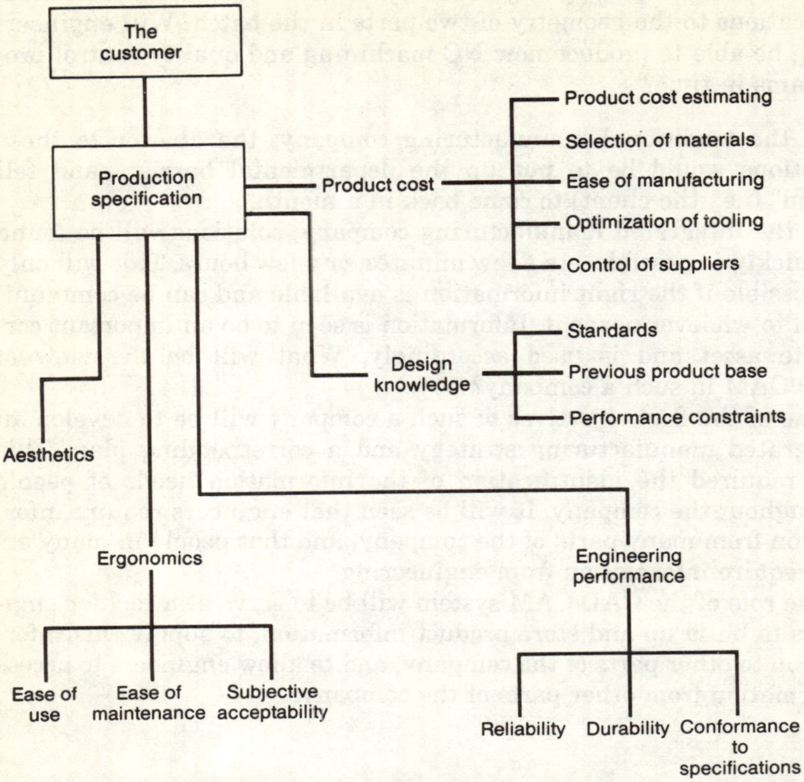

Figure 1.1 Some important design parameters.

and engineering managers is to control "change to specification." Changes arise from a variety of sources.

1. The customer or marketing department changes its mind.
2. Parallel design activity resulting from compressed lead times induces change because disciplines are out of step.
3. Some changes are forced on design teams as prototype testing inevitably generates problems which require engineering changes.
4. Manufacturing engineers or production staff discover problems during preproduction or introduction phases.
5. The purchasing department uses alternative suppliers whose products do not meet the entire specification.

The objective for design and engineering managers is to produce a successful product within the shortest possible development time and minimize or control the impact of change.

Into this environment arrives a CAD/CAM salesperson, offering the traditional list of benefits of CAD/CAM, such as increased drafting department productivity, better communications from CAD to CAM, and improved drawing quality. It then becomes the responsibility of the CAD/CAM manager to manage the resource to achieve these benefits. However, none of these benefits appear to affect design engineering. Can CAD/CAM really be used to assist in this task?

Good design management is a matter of

1. Establishing a specification, achieving the right concept, and maintaining the concept during change
2. Setting the cost
3. Establishing the development time scale
4. Monitoring targets
5. Establishing the design/engineering organization

Over the last 5 years new disciplines and new philosophies have matured. These include design to cost, design for manufacture, computer-aided engineering, right-first-time engineering, and design for quality. These seem more important to the design manager than CAD/CAM.

Basically a CAD/CAM system does not directly improve the management of design and engineering functions, but it can act as a catalyst for improvement in skills, training, organization, planning, and procedures. If CAD/CAM does not directly help manage the design process, can it assist in designing and engineering? Perhaps. It can provide some useful tools. However, CAD/CAM is often mismanaged, and CAD/CAM only helps if it is well managed and the tools are used effectively. Three-dimensional modeling can improve visual analysis, tool path checking, assembly, and packaging. Computer analysis can help to reduce the time required for prototype testing. Design databases can make it easier to reuse existing designs. Design history documentation and change control can make it easier to find information and to make sure that changes are recorded.

To sum up, good design is reflected in good products. Good products come from a well-managed design organization. A well-managed design function needs to have a multidisciplinary approach. In a well-managed organization, resources are used effectively. CAD/CAM is just a tool for designers to help them in visualizing, testing, and controlling designs. It is often a mismanaged tool. Were it managed better, it might be more useful.

1.8 CAD/CAM—The Electronic Engineer's View

Figure 1.2 should help to show how we use CAD/CAM. We start off with a block diagram functional approach. Then we use the computer-aided engineering (CAE) system to create schematic designs. The system has a really helpful library of electronic functions and symbols—it has all the common transistor-transistor logic (TTL) complementary metal oxide silicon (CMOS) circuits, and we have enhanced it a lot

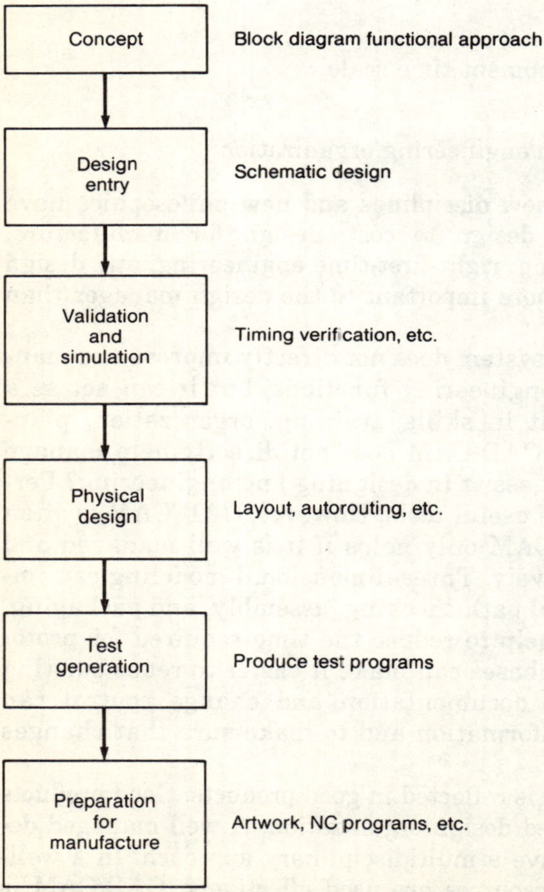

Figure 1.2 CAD/CAM and the electronic engineer.

with our own definitions. The system has powerful circuit logic and analog simulation facilities which provide us with an alternative to breadboarding for testing the design to required performance levels. We can simulate all sorts of dc and ac functions, step frequency, bandwidth, and so on. A very comprehensive color graphics display of parameters such as gain and phase shift helps us interpret the output from simulation runs. By applying failure rates of the individual components, we can estimate how reliable a new product will be and what effect failure of a particular component will have on product operation. Then we have a printed circuit board (PCB) design software package that helps us to create good board layouts with the right characteristics for manufacturing. Our system has autoplacement, multilayer autorouting, and design rule checking. The documentation for manufacturing is produced using the schematic layout package and a drawing system. This alone saves countless hours and eliminates all sorts of transcription errors. We use CAE to generate all sorts of things to speed up the manufacturing process. It does photoplotter artwork, test pattern input for ATE, input data for ACI, and NC drill drive tapes. It gives us a complete parts list that gets passed on to purchasing and production planners. We really like the system, and we've just asked our CAD/CAM manager for advice on upgrading it.

1.9 CAD/CAM—The Drafter's View

A few years ago, we went to some meetings where the engineering manager told us that the company was thinking about introducing CAD/CAM. For a while after that nothing happened, then suddenly four of us were sent to a course to learn how to use a CAD/CAM system. It was a 1-week course, and at the end of it I was exhausted and depressed. Exhausted because I had got out of the habit of learning new things, and in that course there really were a lot of new things to learn. Depressed because I felt that I didn't make such good progress as the other three; I kept forgetting things and making mistakes.

However, once the system was installed in the company I gradually got into the habit of using it. Working at the screen is quite enjoyable when you get used to it. There are times when you can work really fast because the system does a lot of things for you. Another good thing is that we often have to design something with the system. That never used to happen. It turns out that I'm quite good at design, and I may soon be promoted.

There are problems with the system, but no one ever does anything about them. We have eight screens in an open-plan room, and often it's difficult to concentrate when designers and managers come in and start talking about the work. In the summer, the sun shines directly onto four of the screens, and it's almost impossible to work on them. By the time the CAD/CAM manager gets round to doing anything about it, winter's with us and the problem has gone. And then there's the plotter. To save money they bought a small plotter, so we still have to do big plots by hand. That's a real pain.

1.10 CAD/CAM—The Accountant's View

Yesterday, I had to check out a proposal for a CAD/CAM system. Those guys down in engineering must have been kidding me. They were asking for an investment of $4 million, and when I worked out the figures, it turned out that the payback period was 5 years, Yes, 5 years! Where do those guys think they are? This is Detroit, not somewhere in southeast Asia. Don't those guys realize that an investment of $4 million would put our Q3 figures in the red? Our share price would drop, and we'd have all Wall Street on our backs. Why don't they wake up to the realities of the world? One day those loonies down there want machine tools, the next it's computers, networks, CAD/CAM, and I don't know what else. Why should I approve their CAD/CAM request? I'd never even heard of it before yesterday.

1.11 CAD/CAM—The Lexicographer's View

Should it be CAD or CADD or CAD/CAM or CADCAM or CAE or MCAE or what?

When we look back over history we can generally identify how and why a word got its meaning. We understand why the meat of a pig is not called pig, but pork. Similarly with people's names. We know where names such as Hill, Schuster, and Smith came from.

The problem with these CAD-related acronyms is that they don't have centuries of history behind them, nor is there any international body to standardize them. As a result everyone interprets them differently. This leads to quite a lot of confusion. When companies first get involved in CAD/CAM there's always a lot of misunderstanding about the degree of computer aid that is going to be received. Some people think the "D" in CAD is for design, others think it's for drafting. Some think CAD includes manufacturing engineering and that the CAM in CAD/CAM refers to production planning and factory automation.

CAD/CAM means computer-aided design engineering and computer-aided manufacturing engineering. This is really the same as saying computer-aided engineering—CAE. However, as CAE was first applied to electronics, some people think it is necessary to distinguish "CAE for mechanical engineering" by calling it MCAE.

Probably, in time, all these acronyms will disappear. Computers will be used for all tasks, so there will be no need to talk about computer-aided this and that. In the meantime, the need is to make sure that the system users and managers understand the concepts and don't get confused and upset by misunderstanding the acronyms.

Of course, I may be biased. As a lover of the English language I fervently believe that most of the verbiage that is word-smithed by CAD/CAM experts should be trashed.

1.12 CAD/CAM—The ex-CAD/CAM Manager's View

About 18 months ago I was asked to become CAD/CAM manager. I hadn't been involved in the selection process, but the design office manager said that didn't matter. He told me that he thought I had a lot of future, and if I could handle this one, then I should be in for quick promotion. In that kind of situation you can't do much else apart from accept, and that's what I did.

I really don't know if I resigned or I was asked to resign, but I just couldn't take it anymore. It was a terrible experience—18 months of frustration, pressure, antagonism, back-stabbing, cowardice.... You name it, we had it. Two of the people in my CAD/CAM team supported me and behaved properly. As for the rest, from the CEO down to the shop floor, there's not one person involved in CAD/CAM who I could trust now. "Management," if you can call it that, shirked its responsibilities every time. Most of them believe they can manage things they don't understand. My experience is that they can't. Maybe they can in the military/industrial complex, but not in a small consumer-oriented company like ours. The ones with the MBAs are the worst. Those guys have really destroyed manufacturing in this country. We have more MBAs than ever—and the biggest trade deficit ever. I can forgive the engineers, the drafters, and the analysts and programmers whom I crossed swords with on CAD/CAM—they are technical people and invariably have short-sighted, biased viewpoints. The ones I can't forgive are the managers—they don't understand what CAD/CAM is, and they can't be bothered to learn, so of course it doesn't work.

1.13 Conflicting Views of CAD/CAM—The CAD/CAM Manager's Problem

At first glance, CAD/CAM appears to be a simple productivity improvement tool that is applied to engineering activities. There is a feeling that, like an NC machine tool, it can be quickly chosen, installed, and set to work. Unfortunately, as the CAD/CAM manager will soon discover, this is not so.

CAD/CAM is a technique for improving the flow, quality, and use of engineering information. Unlike a NC machine tool, it affects many people throughout the company. Unlike the NC machine tool, its "output" is not highly visible. Unlike the NC machine tool, it will not be immediately productive. All the ingredients are in place for a fiasco, and often a fiasco is the result.

However, CAD/CAM has tremendous potential for improving engineering productivity. The CAD/CAM manager must not cease to believe this but must accept that others need to be shown that it is so. Successful implementation of CAD/CAM is just as much a question of organization, people, and planning as it is of technology. It is not enough to have pretty pictures on the screen. The CAD/CAM manager must ensure that the expectations of people in the company are understood and translated into mutually agreed-upon requirements. These requirements must be met by the system, or there must be plans to meet these requirements by an agreed-upon date.

Chapter 2

Planning and Control of the CAD/CAM Project

The CAD/CAM manager is responsible for the introduction and everyday administration of CAD/CAM. This is a complex task. It takes a long time and uses a lot of resources. In later chapters, the individual activities are detailed, but first it is useful to review the necessary requirements for planning and controlling a complex project of this type.

2.1 The Need for a Business Plan

Manufacturing organizations generally have a departmental structure. Financial parameters and other key indicators are reported along departmental lines by the accounting function. In the financial reports that are periodically produced, the figures usually show very clearly how each department has been performing relative to its targets.

A desire to improve the accounting figures on a departmental basis usually lies behind projects undertaken within the traditional manufacturing organization. There is strong motivation within such a structure to generate projects which primarily affect the results of a given department. Many CAD/CAM projects have been undertaken on this basis. The CAD equipment is installed to reduce drafting time and thus reduce the payroll of the drafting department. A numerically controlled milling machine is installed to improve the efficiency of the "milling department."

Most manufacturing organizations know how to plan and control projects of the type just mentioned—projects which are justified within the purview of each department and which primarily affect the future accounting results for that department. A series of such projects leads to the "islands of automation" phenomena in which the information available from each "island" must be humanly interfaced to other islands. Although it is not surprising that initial moves toward CAD/CAM have occurred in islands, it is generally agreed that CAD/CAM can deliver much more than departmental efficiency.

This chapter is not primarily intended to address the planning and control of departmental projects, although the principles developed here are certainly applicable to those projects. Rather, this chapter addresses the more complex methods that must be applied if CAD/CAM is to deliver its full potential. The reasons for the added complexity have already been hinted at. To deliver their full potential, CAD/CAM projects have to cross established organizational and accounting boundaries. Many of the possible benefits of CAD/CAM arise from the elimination of error-prone, time-consuming, and unsystematic methodologies in use at departmental interfaces. Actions leading to improvements in these areas will affect the organizational and the financial overhead structures of the organization. If real benefits are to result from the CAD/CAM project, the contents of many tasks will have to change, and some may well disappear.

Major CAD/CAM strategies will affect the whole company. These strategies have to be planned and agreed to at very senior levels. The level of agreement must include the person who has full responsibility for all departments which will be affected in a major way by proposed changes. Since these will almost inevitably involve changes in the reporting of financial and operational parameters (as well as expected improvements in the operating results), the level of approval needed almost inevitably rests with top management. In view of the interdepartmental repercussions, top management must also be involved with the planning and must, to some considerable extent, drive the planning function.

The best vehicle for driving major changes is the business plan. Business planning methodologies have been described in many publications and will not be dwelt on at length here. It is sufficient to say that the importance of a business plan to an organization's future rises very sharply as the time constant associated with its business dynamics shortens. When changes are made relatively seldom, are relatively small, or tend not to cross departmental boundaries, there is little need to spend extensive effort in discussing the nature of these changes and documenting them in a business plan. However, when changes come more frequently, or are large and cross departmental boundaries, as is the case with CAD/CAM, a more formal business planning document is needed to promote consistency of action.

CAD/CAM technologies have reached sufficient maturity that their effects upon a business organization can be reasonably quantified. It is therefore possible for management to reap the benefits of CAD/CAM on a companywide basis without prior experimentation with isolated islands of automation. As soon as a companywide approach to CAD/CAM can be developed, the chosen approach should be reflected in the business plan.

The CAD/CAM entry in the business plan will identify the general business areas most appropriate for CAD/CAM and state the company objective in each area. The scope of CAD/CAM application will be defined and its links to other systems, both manual and computerized, identified. Planned benefits and costs will be defined and stated in tangible terms. Organizational issues will be addressed. Preparation of the plan may be a painstaking process, but once it is developed and accepted, the plan becomes an excellent tool first for gaining the necessary resources and then for managing them.

A companywide approach to CAD/CAM can only be developed following a systematic review of the possibilities. In a medium-sized organization such a review is neither long nor arduous. In very large organizations, a review can take several months to perform. A major CAD/CAM project is bound to stretch the capabilities of any organization—large or small. Its widespread impact means the project is bound to appear large and complex relative to other projects. In all probability, a CAD/CAM project of typical size will stretch the availability of talented company staff to execute it. On the other hand, it is unlikely that such a project will strain the financial resources of the company.

Any CAD/CAM project requires a considerable contribution in thoughtful analysis by senior people. Any successful plan will contain some elements of flexibility because there will always be some elements of the unknown. For success, there must be considerable determination at senior levels to make the plan become an operational reality on budget and on time. The likelihood of being able to achieve these goals is very significantly enhanced by making an early investment in project planning.

2.2 In Search of Opportunity

Change for its own sake is not necessarily cost-effective. One of the first objectives in planning a CAD/CAM project must be to find out in which areas CAD/CAM will be cost-effective in a particular business situation. CAD/CAM can be used to attain different types of business improvement. Some areas will be particularly fruitful for particular types of opportunity, others will have little to offer.

As is shown in more detail in Chapter 4, the primary reasons for undertaking a CAD/CAM project can only be cost reduction, increase in sales turnover (leading to market share improvement), or some combination of the two. It is important that the project planners understand the fundamental business reasons for the project and the way in which the benefits of the project will be brought to the balance sheet. If the focus is to be on market share improvement, then such parameters as product quality, the interval from customer order to customer delivery, or the time interval from design start to sample product sale are important. When the focus is to be on product cost reduction, then parameters such as the cost of quality, direct cost of labor and/or material, and the cost of overhead as a percentage of product manufactured costs are important. By choosing to focus CAD/CAM activity on achieving improved values on selected business parameters, management can significantly shorten many of the debates that are likely to occur during the selection of a CAD/CAM solution. Alternatives can be compared on the basis of the extent to which these contribute to improvement of the selected business parameters. Opportunity lies in the improvement of selected business parameters.

The importance of CAD/CAM as a technique to improve the quality, flow, and use of engineering information has already been mentioned. The CAD/CAM world is "information intensive." The value of information to a business organization has always been high, but in the past the costs of gathering information have been so high that "information intensive" operations were rarely cost-effective. However, appropriately configured CAD/CAM operations are capable of gathering information very cheaply. The economic balance is shifting in favor of information intensive operations. No longer does information gathering have to conjure up images of the completion of endless forms in multiple copies, clerical staff dedicated to data reduction, draftspeople drawing charts, and monthly management meetings centered upon the dutiful review of outdated facts. Mechanisms for the automatic gathering, formatting, and presentation of very current information are here to stay and constitute a significant tool in the cost-effective management of today's dynamic enterprises. Automatic gathering of information should be part of any CAD/CAM project. This is an opportunity.

In order to prevent the development of a new "island of information" after CAD/CAM is introduced, it is necessary to look beyond the boundaries of the engineering function. In many manufacturing concerns the most information intensive operation is manufacturing resource planning (MRP). Significant amounts of information are needed to set up a successful MRP II installation. When accurate information is not available, management must make assumptions and at least temporarily build these assumptions into the MRP II database. On the other hand, a well-installed MRP II system generates a lot of information with which to update or correct bad initial assumptions. Properly administered, the package provides information needed for its controllers to target and track future waste reduction activity. The CAD/CAM system can provide high-quality information for MRP. The MRP system can provide useful information, such as product and parts costs and availabilities, for engineers. In many organizations the link between CAD/CAM and MRP is likely to provide a further opportunity to improve business parameters.

Similarly, the interfaces to activities in other departmental areas can often offer significant opportunities. Improvement of information flow with production (for example, NC machine data) or with marketing (for example, data for quotes) are typical of these.

CAD/CAM projects are unlikely to be cash positive in the short term. One exception to this arises when some element of CAD/CAM leads to a significant inventory reduction. In these cases—and it can only happen once—the cash flow generated by the inventory reduction can significantly reduce the negative cash flow demands of the major hardware and software purchase associated with CAD/CAM activity. Net cash inflow is not a likely short-term opportunity.

CAD/CAM will be useful to a company that applies it for well-identified reasons. The manufacturing company will need significant information about the business in order to formulate plans. A major CAD/CAM plan which is to avoid the islands of automation phenomena must address the engineering/manufacturing interface, the information demands of various CIM technologies, the information generating capabilities of each technology, and the business needs for this information.

To successfully select an appropriate CAD/CAM opportunity, a manufacturing management team has to know a lot about the operation which it manages. An operations review can produce the required information.

2.3 The Operations Review

A major CAD/CAM project is going to produce many changes throughout the organization. These changes will cross departmental boundaries and lead to the restructuring of departments and the redefinition of many jobs. The perceived contribution of various departments to the financial success of the company will change.

In order to plan changes of this magnitude, a common understanding of the "as is" situation is needed. Only from this common basis can the company be repartitioned and rebalanced when new equipment and methods are introduced.

A manufacturing company that is of sufficient size to consider the use of CAD/CAM will necessarily be a complex operation. Management seldom has a thorough or widely held and common understanding of the interrelationships between departments. For example, if a company can achieve a shorter material dwell time in manufacturing, what are the resulting overhead savings due to corresponding reductions in error, breakage, and spoilage? In what departments will these savings occur? Where will these savings show up in the financial results? What has to be done within the organization in order to move these predicted savings to the balance sheet?

An effective way of obtaining the basic information needed for an effective discussion of such issues is to perform an operations review. The technique is described in more detail in Chapter 6. It is briefly described here within the context of the development of the overall CAD/CAM project plan. Although there are usually many individuals available within a company with the necessary knowledge and background to perform such a review, these individuals can seldom be spared from their current operational duties to perform the required data gathering and analysis. Employment of a temporary outside resource (such as a management consultant) is usually the only reasonable alternative.

The operations review should produce a description of the "as is" situation, and of the competitive situation in the marketplace for the product group to which it is proposed to apply CAD/CAM methods. It should also describe the "to be" situation with emphasis on operational opportunities of the sort already described and give an assessment of the operational-managerial environment.

Since CAD/CAM will be implemented to reduce costs and/or increase market share, the review of the competitive situation looks for needs and opportunities in these areas. Is price a very sensitive issue? Can market share be increased by shortening the customer order to customer delivery interval? Would market position be enhanced by providing more options or features within the product line? Useful answers to these questions can probably be obtained by interviewing several members of the management team, formulating a preliminary position on the issues, and then holding a group discussion of this draft position with selected members of the management group. Data are gathered, their accuracy is tested through discussion, and then some consensus listing the opportunities in the competitive situation can be generated.

Investigation of the operational opportunities is a more numerically oriented activity than the competitive situation analysis. In this portion of the review, the overall engineering sequence is documented. To the extent possible, costs and value added are attributed to each operation. The causes of losses resulting from delays and queuing, the costs of checking, and the costs of rework are identified. To the extent possible, significant changes in methods and costs during recent history are documented. The number of existing part and process descriptions should be noted. The annual number of new and modified products should be identified. Again, the objective is to gather information and to obtain a broad-based consensus that is sufficiently accurate for the purpose of defining CAD/CAM opportunity.

Finally, the operational review must generate some comments on the managerial-operational environment. The main issue here is the acceptability of risk taking and change in the established environment. The extent to which individuals are identified with past successes and failures will be noted. The history of other major projects in the company will be examined.

Any significant move toward the introduction of CAD/CAM will constitute a major change. A change of this magnitude can only be accomplished within an organization which is not overly averse to risk and which, to some noticeable extent, rewards success. Either this environment must exist at the outset of the CAD/CAM undertaking or there must be determination at the top of the company to achieve this environment before significant investment in time and money is made.

Once the operational review has been completed and the findings agreed upon, the organization will have gained considerable consensus about where its opportunities lie. It will have tentatively identified some specific projects. The organization will be ready to generate a plan.

2.4 Generating a Plan and Launching It

The process of generating a plan for a major change is not entirely independent of the process of "selling" the plan. The iterative process of generating the plan helps to test its acceptability to the senior managers who will eventually have to approve it. Every opportunity should be taken to test and "presell" the major parameters of the plan such as cost, timing, and expected payback.

Any complex plan will consist of several nested subplans at varying levels of detail. There is no need to generate the details of the lowest levels of the plan prior to seeking its formal acceptance. However, it is essential from the outset to identify the key results or business parameter changes that will be achieved by implementing the plan. It is these values that are of most importance to management.

Any complex plan which is characterized by several levels of uncertainty is best planned, presented, and monitored as a series of interim events characterized by specified dates on which specified sums of money will have been expended. These events are termed "milestones." The milestones should be "binary." A binary milestone is an event in time which must be described in such a way that it is definitively either met or not met by the specified date. For example, "RFP released to prospective suppliers" is a binary milestone. It will be clear on the milestone's due date whether the RFP has been released. On the other hand, the same milestone stated as "High-quality RFP released to prospective suppliers" is not a binary milestone because there is no way to measure the quality of the RFP document and thereby state whether the milestone was met. Similarly, the milestone "software 80 percent coded" is not a binary milestone because nobody can definitively say whether the 80 percent point has been reached.

Milestones should exist for both internal and external activities (such as delivery of equipment). The binary milestone is not particularly useful in planning a project (and later in monitoring it) unless the financial expenditures expected by the date of each achievement are simultaneously stated. By tying achievement to expenditures, all aspects of the project, except for the quality of the products, will be defined. To the extent that quality can be defined numerically, it too can be built into binary milestones. However, it must be admitted that because of the nature of the uncertainties in many complex projects, and the resulting tradeoffs in many aspects of quality, the predefinition of many quality measures is counterproductive. The quality issues may best be left to the professionalism of those involved in the project. Experience shows that a team which is essentially delivering binary milestones on time and on budget is generally also delivering a quality product.

Each milestone must be "owned" by somebody; otherwise it will not be met on time. The date of the milestone should be scheduled by this person with assistance if necessary from the project manager. Ideally, the owner should have full responsibility and adequate control of the necessary resources to ensure delivery. However, it is unlikely that the control will be absolute, and successful managers of complex projects must learn to be reasonably comfortable while operating without absolute control.

On a complex project, no individual can own more than about 12 milestones with due dates in the same year. Thus, the number of milestones which can be usefully generated for a project is defined by the number of owners available. The temptation to generate an excessive number of milestones relative to this measure indicates either an attempt at overly constraining a dynamic project or a serious shortage of resources available to execute the project. Either situation is dangerous to the success of the project. For certain tasks assigned to less skilled people it may be necessary to develop more frequent milestones so that performance can be more closely monitored.

A manager who owns (i.e., has responsibility for) a milestone may legitimately have considerable interest in the progress being made toward related milestones. Thus it is useful to develop a table that shows each milestone, its owner, and who has an interest in it. For each individual in a project team, it is fairly easy to show which milestones are owned and which are of interest. A simple guideline on this issue might be that a manager has an interest in the milestones owned by individuals one or two levels below in the company hierarchy. Certainly, other guidelines can be developed as appropriate.There should always be room for expressing legitimate interest in milestones outside of an individual's own organization when their achievement critically affects one owned by that individual. An individual who has an interest in a milestone should be kept informed of progress being made toward meeting that milestone on time. Correspondingly, an individual who owns a milestone has to inform others of the progress made toward its achievement.

The project management structure just described not only defines the project, but also defines both responsibilities and interests in the project. This technique is valuable during the planning phases of a project and, as will be seen later, is extremely valuable in tracking progress against expectations. On large projects, it also constitutes an invaluable tool for keeping the project on track as project personnel are changed. When an individual leaves a project, the milestones owned are readily identifiable and obviously new owners must be found for them. When a new individual joins the project, responsibility is immediately defined by assignment of ownership of appropriate milestones, and interests are defined by formally recording the milestones that are of interest but not owned.

The task of keeping track of milestone ownership and the interested parties associated with each milestone is not onerous. Changes in the assignment of ownership and of interests over time are easily tracked using today's tools. The effort is easily justified by the continued focus which it brings to the project and those responsible for it.

The milestone planning technique constitutes a ready-made reporting tool. However, there are two further planning issues to be considered, namely the organization for financial reporting and the strategy for winning over the doubters by proving early success. The first issue is usually resolved more easily than the second.

In most organizations, mechanisms already exist for the establishment of new categories of expenses. The CAD/CAM project will need an expense account and probably several subaccounts. Consideration should be given to setting up accounts partitioned by work activity, rather than along the lines of existing departments. Presumably, existing mechanisms will provide the departmental information anyway, while appropriately chosen subaccounts, which focus on selected project activities, will aid considerably in controlling and changing budget allocations as the project progresses.

Risks and expenses can be minimized by tackling what appear to be the most difficult parts of the project first. If major unforeseen problems are to surface, they will probably surface in these areas. Once they have been resolved, the way is clear for a smooth run into project completion. However, focusing on the most difficult tasks first is also likely to produce some early signs of failure, whereas some early signs of success would be preferable. In an organization which does not measure up strongly for its tolerance to change, early success may be essential. For these reasons, some element of the CAD/CAM project which is likely to be easily achievable and yet reasonably impressive should be specifically scheduled for early accomplishment.

Finally, just before submitting a plan for senior approval, it should be subjected to several "gross tests of reasonableness." When a plan is prepared it often happens that the estimate of the total is calculated as the sum of identified parts. This method of estimation tends to underestimate the total for two reasons. First, it assigns neither time nor expense to unidentified parts. Second, it seldom takes into account interactions between the various parts of the project, and these interactions are much more likely to lead to delay and additional expense than to the opposite tendency. Gross tests of reasonableness enable the planners to stand back and see whether the whole plan falls within a generally accepted and reasonable framework. Consider the following "gross tests of reasonableness." Does the total predicted expenditure divided by the number of working days available to the project yield a manageable daily expenditure rate? Was there an earlier project with a similar daily rate of expenditure, and have plans been made to avoid the major problems which were encountered on that project? For part-time senior people, what percentage of their time has been allotted to this project? What tasks will these people give up in order to make the time available? Is it understood how engineering will carry out its day-to-day tasks during the transition period from a manual to a CAD/CAM environment? Have costs been included for overlapping production periods? Has a reasonable yield profile and equipment uptime profile during start-up been assumed? Has the published literature been checked for comments about similar projects?

With the checks for completeness and reasonableness accomplished, it is time to seek formal approval. A presentation of some sort is almost always required. The style of presentation will depend upon the norms of the organization, but the following two points should be considered.

1. It is best to build an understanding of the issues on the project and to seek some acceptance of the risk involved at the time the project is approved, rather than getting into these areas for the first time if and when the project is experiencing problems.
2. Secondly, in some cases it may be necessary to secure the approval of very senior management for the appointment of the project team leader. If that is the case, approval for that appointment should be sought simultaneously with approval of the plan itself.

With formal approval secured, the project can be formally launched. People subordinate to the project leader will be assigned, and in most cases these assignments will come as no great surprise because many of those people will probably have been involved during project planning. Detailed project planning can start only after the major responsibilities have been allocated. Just before making these appointments the project manager should again consider the issues of technology, personnel, and the environment. Factors relevant to these issues may indeed have changed significantly during the planning interval. The planning activity itself may have affected some of these issues. These activities will also have revealed hitherto unknown strengths, weaknesses, and interests of some of the individuals involved during the planning phases.

Any manager of a complex project soon realizes that securing the formal approval for the financial resources was by far the easiest part of the start-up. Almost inevitably, the most difficult part is securing the services of the internal personnel who are to participate on the project. No manager is likely to get everything hoped for in this regard. This may lead to an increase in project risks. It is important that the project manager understand this and make moves to reduce those rising risks. Unfortunately, this action is most likely to lead to the delay of some parts of the project. If this is the case, it is best to reschedule early since such a move does the least damage to project team credibility.

Securing external resources, while time consuming and somewhat prone to delay, is nevertheless a fairly straightforward task. Equally, the necessity for external acquisition of personnel should have been allowed for in the project plan and supported by the necessary financial commitment.

2.5 Managing Technology and People

The cardinal rule of implementation planning is "do not unnecessarily compound the risks." In any portion of the project, relatively safe elements should be combined with any particularly risky one. The combination of several risky elements often results in the project getting out of control. Software is likely to be a major problem and can be used to illustrate this point. Not more than one major unproven software element should be used, even when major well-known suppliers are involved. An unproven software team should not be used to develop software at unproven interfaces. Features of "proven" software which have not been used on prior installations should be identified and not used in a new hardware environment.

Some of the same thought processes about not compounding the technological risks can be applied to personnel selection as well. It is important that some of the key personnel be internally credited with having successfully executed a major project before. Even if these individuals are not thought to be the strongest technical candidates, they really know how to make things work in the company. Their talents in these directions will stand the project in good stead when difficulties arise. In each section of the organization and at each level, risks can be reduced by seeking personnel appointments which complement each other, rather than back up or duplicate each other.

Regardless of how good the environment is regarding willingness to accept risk and change, serious consideration should be given to implementation of a specific reward scheme for such a major and critical project. Of course, if a performance-based reward scheme already exists within the company, performance on this project can be tied to that scheme. In either case, the risk-reward environment with respect to this project needs to be specifically addressed. Everything reasonable should be done to encourage the project team to take risks where justified and then to work their way around the obstacles they encounter. Opportunities for success are rarely risk-free.

Finally, in regard to gathering and committing resources for the project, mention must be made of the issues of internal accommodations. These issues are seldom addressed early enough and are very often the source of both project delay and acrimonious recrimination within a management team. For example, the CAD/CAM project will often affect engineering and manufacturing schedules. The magnitude of this impact has to be discussed early, and the details of the impact must be worked out before it seriously compromises schedules. It should be remembered that some parts of the organization will see all this as an imposition, and the issue must be handled accordingly.

There may be a requirement to build inventory of either raw material or finished goods to hedge against a possible or planned manufacturing schedule disruption due to the installation of some aspect of CAD/CAM. If inventory is to be built, then inventory build has to be planned and those responsible for inventory control have to be "forgiven" the inventory bulge which results. Again, unless the issue is properly handled, those responsible for inventory control will see this issue as an imposition on them.

In some cases there will be pricing, product availability, or advertising issues associated with the CAD/CAM project. An ongoing interface between the project team and the marketing organization is essential in these cases. Because of the risks being undertaken in the CAD/CAM project, clear paths of communication have to be established with the marketing organization so that if there are delays with the CAD/CAM project, the necessary accommodations are made within marketing. Again, there are many ways to get this wrong.

2.6 Project Control

The process of project control should always focus on the achievement of the primary objectives in the plan's future. Intermediate objectives may be sacrificed or compromised, but management must be continually aware of the forward risks and know what its options are. If management's attention is focused on the two rules which follow, this will be the case.

1. It is necessary to continually assess the likelihood of achieving future milestones on time and on budget. The reason for doing this is not only to maintain focus on the primary objectives, but also to warn others who might be affected by changes in project schedules so that they too can optimize their forward plans.
2. It is necessary to gather the information required for replanning the project as problems develop or new opportunities arise.

With these rules guiding their actions, management will avoid the pitfall of focusing attention primarily upon detailed reporting of events of the recent past. This all too traditional style of reporting is time consuming, primarily self-serving by the management team, and of little value to the project. Events are not necessarily achievements, and unless past events are important to the understanding of the forward risks or options, little time or effort should be spent on reporting them.

Progress reporting can be either written or verbal, but some written reporting is essential. Reporting should always be relative to project milestones. The frequency of reporting should be determined by the time frame of the milestones being considered. Specifically, the frequency of reporting should reflect the time interval at which those reporting would be expected to manage the project unguided. At the lowest level, the reporting interval might be weekly, whereas at senior levels project reporting might be quarterly.

Reports, regardless of frequency, should focus on a current evaluation of the likelihood of meeting future milestones. Additionally, milestones which have actually been achieved—whether on time or not—should be recorded. Finally, suggestions or current activities aimed at overcoming project problems should be recorded. Written reports should be brief and should be produced by milestone owners about their own milestones. Ideally, milestone reports should only go to those who are listed as having an interest in them.

Project reporting should not be done by clerically oriented staff who produce reports as a result of superficial contact with milestone owners. Reports produced in this manner lack credibility and thus degrade the whole reporting process. The interactions between various milestones are seldom really understood by clerically oriented reporters, and thus project jeopardies are not caught soon enough for effective remedial action. The other inherent problem in the clerical approach to progress reporting arises because the importance of various milestones to overall project success is far from equal. Clerically oriented reporting tends to assume equality, and this again depreciates the value of the reporting document in the eyes of project management. Project management has to be taken seriously. It cannot be delegated. It has to be performed—and seen to be performed—by the milestone owners.

There is a need for formal project report meetings. The manner in which these meetings are run is very important to the climate of the project. The main purpose of the meeting has to be to share relevant information in an atmosphere which promotes cross-questioning as a means of refining that information. The meeting should first gather the facts. In doing so, it should avoid detailed descriptions of current activity and should insist upon each individual making a statement about milestones owned. This process recommits the team to future achievement, and this recommitment is made in the presence of the individuals' subordinates, peers, and superiors. In the face of repeated recommitments, few professionals will do less than their best to bring these commitments to fruition. This process also promotes openness, and it forces milestone owners to use informal means of gathering the information upon which to base their prognosis.

Following the information gathering and prognosis, the meeting may need to be reconstituted as an informal replanning session. Open discussion should be encouraged on how the jeopardies can be minimized. Properly managed, this process can be a potent team-building session.

While it is unnecessary to record minor changes to the project plan which may emerge during the replanning session, care has to be taken that no major discrepancies develop between the officially sanctioned project plan and the current intent of project management. Some reissues of the project plan can be expected, but if frequent reissues are needed, the project itself is clearly out of control and a major formal replanning of the project is called for.

By using the methodologies outlined here, project management can simultaneously be demanding but pragmatic. Success is rewarded, the team comes to the rescue of a milestone activity which is in trouble, and milestone owners who are continually in trouble are not tolerated.

During the course of any prolonged project, there will be several personnel changes. Not all of these changes will involve a simple replacement of one individual by another. Tasks will be subdivided and new alignments and combinations of task responsibilities will be relatively frequent. The formal reassignment of milestone ownership in the face of personnel change is essential to the whole project management approach described here.

There are several project planning tools which are useful in recording plans and ensuring consistency among the relationships of milestones, their timing, and total project time requirements. Planning tools should not, however, be considered to have a management role. Software packages can greatly assist in the reissue of project documents, but they do not have knowledge or decision capabilities beyond those of the project management team.

2.7 Project Control Tools

Milestone management in the CAD/CAM environment is relatively simple, and should not require the use of complex project management software tools. The major variables to be considered are the milestones, their scheduled dates, their relationships, their owners, and the names of those who have an interest in them. Figure 2.1 shows a typical format for the detailed milestone description. Figure 2.2 shows on a single time line the major milestones of the project. This format gives a good overview of the project and is suitable for presentation to company management.

Formal planning techniques such as CPM (critical path method)

Milestone	Content	Owner	Date	Interested parties	Notes
0701	Facility prepared	MA	30 March	PJ	
0702	Hardware + software installed	PJ	13 April	MA	
0703	Environment systems OK	MA	27 April	PJ	
0704	System tested	PJ	1 May	MA	
0705	System manager trained	ZF	8 May		(Milestone 0107)
0706	First user trained	ZF	22 May		(Milestone 0108)
0707	Plotter installed	JP	27 May	PJ	
0708	All phase 1 systems ready	PJ	29 May	ZF, RS, PM	
0709	First user free	RS	1 June	PM	
0710	Library complete	RS	29 June	PM	

Figure 2.1 Typical milestone chart format.

Milestone letter	Number	Task	Expenditure (000$)
A	0310	Selection terminated	100
B	0512	Purchase order sent	150
C	0708	All phase 1 systems ready	400
D	1015	Machining center in production	1000
E	1107	Interface to MRP working	1600
F	1310	Performance review complete	2400
G	1501	Phase 3 started	2700

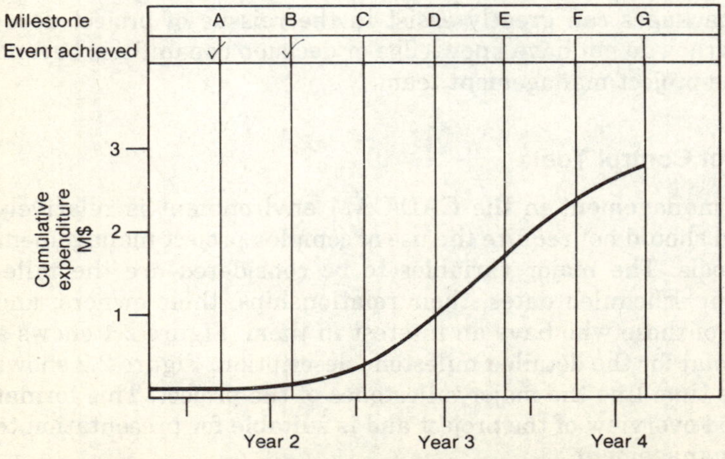

Figure 2.2 Milestone overview.

and PERT (program evaluation and review technique) are generally overkill for controlling this size of project and run the risk of being abandoned after initial enthusiasm runs out. Critical path analysis can help to determine the best initial sequence of tasks and the interrelationship between tasks. Throughout the project, Gantt charts can provide an easily understandable view of the project calendar and personnel assignments.

There are at least 50 project management software packages available. They range in price from about $50 to about $5000. In principle, each of these programs applies techniques to arrange a set of individual tasks that make up the project. However, in practice they differ in many respects: for example, the number of projects, tasks, and people that they can handle. They use different analysis techniques. They track resources (equipment, material, personnel, and money) differently. They vary in the degree to which the expense of tasks and subtasks can be identified. They require different computers and different output devices. Some produce output faster than others; some produce a wider range of output formats.

The objective of CAD/CAM though is not to gain expertise in using project management packages. If the company always uses a particular project management technique, it may want to use it on the CAD/CAM project. If government money is involved, a particular technique or package may be necessary. Otherwise, a very simple package supporting milestone management will be the best solution.

Chapter

3

Organization

3.1 Introduction

All companies, even the smallest, need some sort of organization. An organization is necessary for a variety of reasons, perhaps the most important of which is to manage the company's activities such that its resources are used as effectively as possible in meeting overall company objectives. This is as true for the CAD/CAM resources as it is for the other resources of the company.

The way a company organizes itself for CAD/CAM will depend to some extent on the overall organization of the company. Conversely, the way in which CAD/CAM is implemented can affect the way in which the rest of the company behaves. Unfortunately, the current organization of most companies does not meet the necessary requirements for effective use of CAD/CAM resources. In general, company organizations are still "traditional." They result from a subdivision of work into tasks that can be handled by an individual, a grouping together of related tasks, and the development of communication tasks that pass information and other material between individual tasks. The result is a set of independent noncommunicating empires as shown in Figure 3.1. Figure 3.2, however, shows that from the information point of view the empires are far from independent.

As a result of recent changes in markets, techniques, and tools, such a traditional organization is no longer suitable. An organization that allows CAD/CAM resources to be used as effectively as possible is needed. In product development activities, where CAD/CAM will be used, many changes have occurred. Because of increased competition the market demands lower costs, shorter lead times and product development cycles, and improved quality. It rewards innovative products. The tools available are no longer just pencil and paper, but include computers, graphics screens, and specialized software. Techniques such as design-for-assembly and design-for-manufacturing are receiving wider accep-

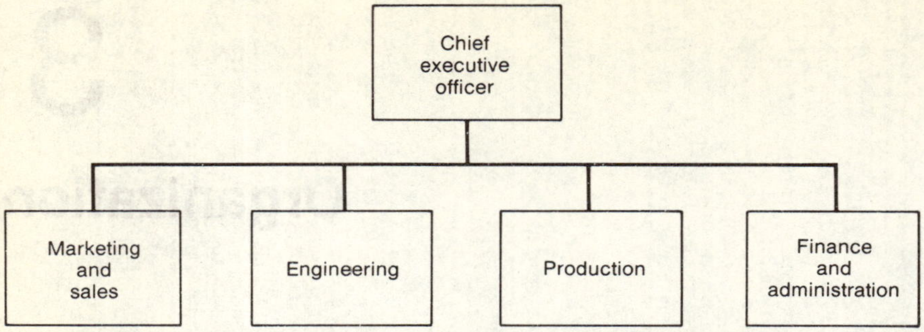

Figure 3.1 The traditional functional organization.

tance. The possibility of reusing, perhaps with slight modifications, designs stored in a CAD/CAM database leads to changes in the way that information is used. Because of all these changes, the tasks of people involved in the product development process are also changing, and a new organizational structure is necessary.

Often the initial decision to work with CAD/CAM is made at a relatively low hierarchic level in the company. At this level, CAD/CAM

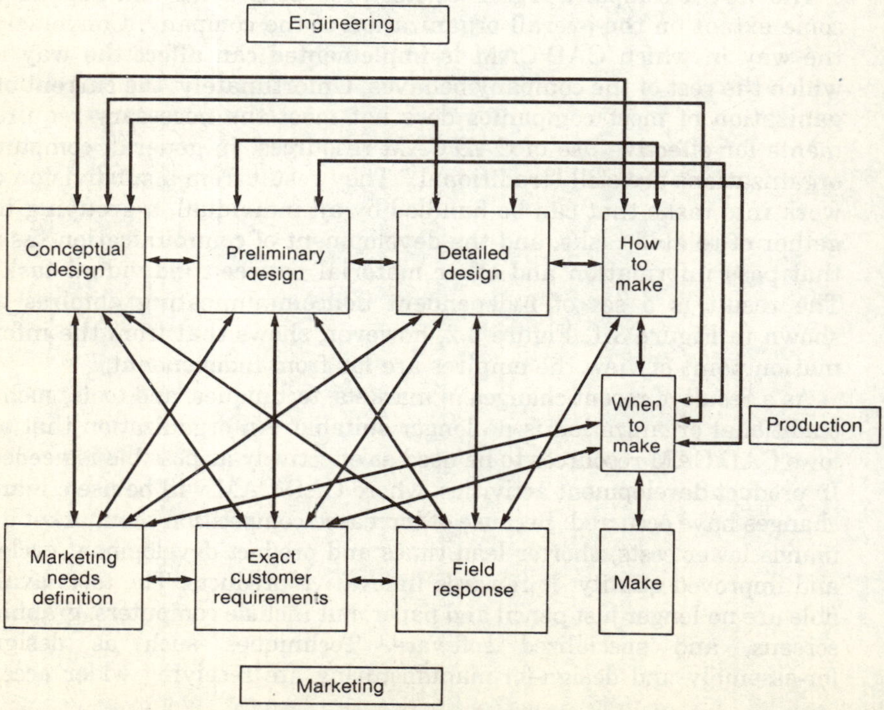

Figure 3.2 Information must flow between functions.

may be regarded as a tool to increase the productivity of drawing production for a particular project. The need to modify the organization is not seen at this point. This is not surprising in the context of the introduction of a new tool to an isolated project. However, as time passes, the use of CAD/CAM spreads to other parts of the product development process, and the changes mentioned in the previous paragraph become more apparent. It becomes clear that the organization must change. As changes are needed throughout the company, they can only be brought about by those who have authority and responsibility for the entire company, i.e., top management. Although others, such as the CAD/CAM manager, the engineering manager, and project managers are responsible for organizing certain activities, they are not responsible for setting up an effective CAD/CAM organization that fits into an overall company organization that reflects a changing environment. This is the responsibility of top management.

Without a real understanding of CAD/CAM and the effect that it can have, top management finds it difficult to develop an effective organization or even to realize that a new organization is necessary. Top management needs to be educated about CAD/CAM before it can make sensible decisions concerning the new organization. Otherwise it may well make mistakes or not get organized at all. One of the most serious mistakes that can be made is to "automate" the existing, traditional organization. This is generally a bad decision as traditional organizations reflect the situation that existed many years ago and, in particular, before the widespread use of computers. They contain too many levels of subdivision, too many discrete, specialized tasks, and communications procedures that are no longer appropriate. Such a decision will not make it easy for the company to achieve the potential benefits of CAD/CAM.

Once implemented, the CAD/CAM organization should provide a framework within which management can plan, direct, and control the use of CAD/CAM so that it can help the company to meet business objectives. The framework helps people to understand what is happening, where they fit, and what they should be doing. At other levels, it helps to prevent duplication of activities and to ensure that standards are maintained.

3.2 Resources

It has been mentioned above that one of the most important functions of an organization is to organize activities in such a way that resources are used as effectively as possible in meeting the business objectives of the company. The major resources that have to be organized in the CAD/CAM context are people, information, equipment, and money. Each of these resources is looked at in detail in later chapters (people in Chapter 5, information in Chapter 8, money in Chapter 4, and selection and day-to-day management of equipment in Chapters 6, 9, and 11).

In the previous section it was mentioned that the organization of CAD/CAM resources eventually becomes a top management responsibility. This chapter aims to help the CAD/CAM manager educate top management so it can understand why this is so and what its role will entail.

3.3 Company Organization

The actual organization in place varies greatly from one company to another and depends on a wide range of factors including industry sector, type of product, volume of production, geographic situation, and number and quality of people employed. To understand the effect of CAD/CAM on the organization, it will be useful to consider a particular example—in this case a company in the mechanical engineering sector.

There are three major functions in the company.

Product development. This part of the company has total responsibility for defining the product and the process by which it will be made. It includes what is traditionally known as design engineering and manufacturing engineering, as well as part of marketing.

Finance and administration.

Production. This part of the company physically makes the product.

Each area has its own resources (people, machines, etc.) which are used "directly" in producing the product, and others which are "support" resources. Each area has its managers, supervisors, and secretaries. Each area has its computer resources.

Traditionally, a company's electronic data processing (EDP) group has often been located in finance and administration. This made sense when the only activities in the company that were computerized were those in finance and administration. However, times have changed, and computers are now used by production and by product development as well as by finance and administration. Production uses computers in production planning and control. CAD/CAM is the major computer-based system used by product development.

In finance and administration, there are people such as the accountant and the pay clerk who use computers, and there is a support group of analysts and programmers (called the EDP group) that is supposed to provide the service required by the users. Similarly, in product development, people like engineers and technicians will use CAD/CAM, and there needs to be a support group (called the CAD/CAM team) that is supposed to provide the service required by the users.

It was stated above that there are four major CAD/CAM resources—people, information, equipment, and money. They are closely linked together. The people involved include the users of the system and the support group (the CAD/CAM team). The equipment is the CAD/CAM system (computer hardware, graphics screens, and software). Users use the equipment to generate information defining the product. Investment of money in equipment and the CAD/CAM team should lead to benefits realized by the users of the equipment.

3.4 The Management of CAD/CAM

At different times, different people at different levels of the company will be responsible for managing the various activities concerning CAD/CAM. This can be illustrated by considering the case of a company that first uses CAD/CAM on a particular project and eventually expands its use to cover all product development activities.

At the beginning there may be just one graphics screen, one computer, and two design engineers using the system. The users would probably be totally responsible for running and using the system. Later, as the use of CAD/CAM grows, there may be 5 screens, 2 computers, and 15 users. A CAD/CAM project manager (probably one of the first users) might be appointed at this time, and another user might be given a part-time job supporting the system. The functions of the CAD/CAM project manager would include organizing the engineering work that is done by the users and being responsible for system support. A CAD/CAM steering committee made up of users' managers and the CAD/CAM project manager may be set up.

The next stage could be 10 screens, 3 computers, and 30 users. By now the CAD/CAM project manager is overworked and torn between design engineering management and CAD/CAM system support management. Many of the users are developing bits of programs to transfer data or to handle special requirements. The engineering department manager does not understand why so much money is being spent or why productivity has not increased. Top management gets involved and finds that two other independent CAD/CAM empires have been built up in the company...In just a few years many companies have gone through this type of experience with the responsibility for CAD/CAM management changing from a project engineer to top management (Figure 3.3).

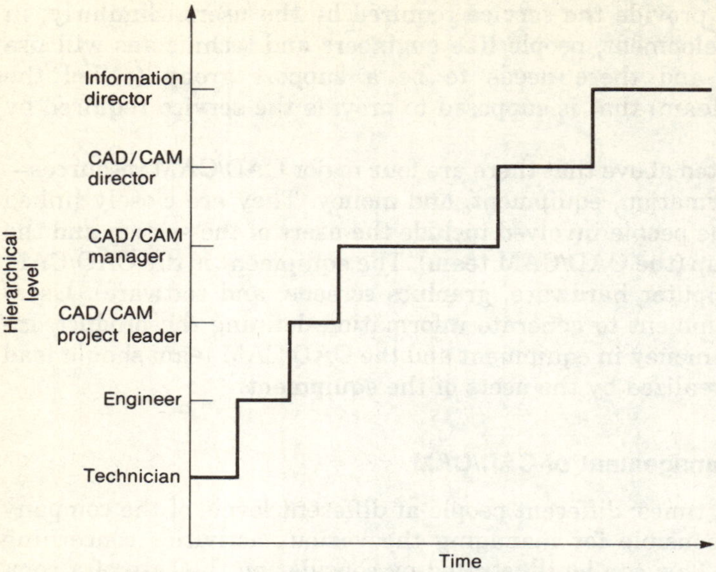

Figure 3.3 The hierarchical level of the person responsible for CAD/CAM increases with time.

If a comparison is made with the finance and administration department, it is often found that the EDP manager (who is responsible for finance and administration computing) reports directly to the finance and administration director. One can foresee that before long a similar situation will arise in product development, where the CAD/CAM manager (responsible for product development computing and information) will report directly to the product development director (responsible for overall product development). Thus, over time, the position in the company hierarchy of the "CAD/CAM manager" rises as CAD/CAM growth occurs. Each new phase sees more resources devoted to CAD/CAM, a change in the form of organization, an increase in the amount of organizational activity associated with CAD/CAM, and an increase in the company's perception of the importance of CAD/CAM.

Unfortunately, these are not the only changes that will be occurring. Even if overall product development activities were to change little, the tools that are used in them, the requirement to access information, the skills and techniques required, the work flow, and the job content of staff will all change. It is quite possible, however, that the overall product development activities will also change fundamentally as a result of the introduction of new technologies.

Unless work in this changing environment is properly organized, it is clear that major problems will occur. Experience shows that very few companies have been able to organize themselves effectively in order to achieve the benefits of CAD/CAM. The most necessary requirement for success is that, right from the beginning, CAD/CAM is the responsibility of one top manager—a person who could be called the CAD/CAM director. Initially such a role is a part-time position. The CAD/CAM director is responsible for seeing that CAD/CAM resources are used effectively and that the transitions between phases of CAD/CAM growth occur smoothly. If all goes well, the CAD/CAM director should be rewarded accordingly. If, however, successful use of CAD/CAM is not achieved, the CAD/CAM director should expect little reward.

Although the hierarchic level and responsibilities of the CAD/CAM manager will change with time, those of the CAD/CAM director will not. The CAD/CAM director needs to be a powerful figure in the company, a good organizer, and a believer in the long-term benefits of CAD/CAM.

3.5 Organizational Form

There is no single organizational form or structure that will always be the best for all companies. As shown above, in a particular company the organization will change with time. There will also be differences between companies in different industrial sectors which result from the relative importance of the product development function. Even in the same industrial sector, the particular organizational form chosen may vary between companies involved in one-of-a-kind or mass production. However, certain general remarks can be made about suitable forms of organization for CAD/CAM.

The best criteria for judging an organizational form is whether it results in objectives being met. The major objective of the CAD/CAM organization is to use engineering information more effectively, thus ensuring that customer requirements are met. An organization that is too rigid will prevent the company from changing to meet the changing environment. An organization that inhibits the free flow of information will also obstruct attempts to be receptive to customer requirements. Engineering information is one of the company's major assets, and there will be those who want to put it under secure, centralized control. However, information is only of value when used, and the users of engineering information are widely spread. They will require access to the information from widely distributed points. Access to information is a major constituent of power. Given information, powerful tools such as CAD/CAM systems, and support from management, the product development staff is well on the way to producing the innovative products required by the market. CAD/CAM must be organized such that the need to control and centralize information (perhaps for reasons of security, integrity, and easier data management) is in balance with those needs to make it widely available.

The organization must clarify the roles of people and groups of people. Authority and responsibility must be defined. It must be clear which groups of people are responsible for which tasks. In the past, this has been less of a problem because the available tools have changed little. However, with the introduction of CAD/CAM, things change; for example, a design engineer may well decide to use CAD/CAM to produce a simple NC tool path. (Does the organization permit this? Where is the program stored? With the design engineer, with the manufacturing engineer, or with whom?) A manufacturing engineer may decide to use CAD/CAM to design a jig for a part and find that the jig would be much easier to make if a minor change was made to the design of the part. (This is a typical example of a "benefit of CAD/CAM" as proposed by a CAD/CAM system vendor. Technologically it is simple, but from the organizational point of view it can quickly lead to chaos.)

Another potential conflict that the organization has to resolve or at least accommodate is that between functional divisions and teams. There are many advantages to a functional organization with, for example, a design office, drawing office, planning office, programming office, quality office, and so on. Each office is expert in its specialty and can easily measure and control its productivity and quality. However, there is often a lack of communication between the offices, with the end result that the final product is not exactly what was intended at the beginning. On the other hand, in a team organization bringing together one specialist from each of the offices to work together on a product, there should (in principle) be no communication problem. In most companies, the organization will have to support both structures, as either may be more appropriate for a given product, phase of CAD/CAM, or set of people. In this case, the organization should try to develop the strengths of both approaches. Thus even when a functional approach is necessary, the organization should aim at removing the walls between different offices and encourage lateral communications between people engaged in different activities.

Lateral communications should be as direct as possible and should bear as little overhead as possible. Organizations with 10 or 20 hierarchic levels make no sense in the CAD/CAM environment. Traditional methods of "communication" between staff in different offices may have involved getting approval at successive vertical levels for an eventual transfer of information at the director level, followed by further rounds of misinterpretation up and down the hierarchic levels. Those days are over. The CAD/CAM organization must define the property and circulation rights of information. Within this framework, a transfer of information requires no more than a status check and then the transfer.

Organizations become "flatter" and job descriptions tend to become broader as unnecessary hierarchic levels are removed. The broadening of job descriptions is partly vertical, resulting from a redistribution of tasks that were originally carried out at many levels among a smaller number of levels (although it may well be found that many of the tasks are no longer needed). It is also partly horizontal; thus, even at a particular level, job descriptions should encourage people to carry out tasks over a similar hierarchic level but in previously separate areas (e.g., the design engineer who uses CAD/CAM to develop tool paths).

Organization is only a means to an end, and that end is the fulfillment of client requirements. An organizational structure cannot develop a solution to a client's request. If it inhibits people from finding that solution, then it is probably not the most suitable structure and (after investigation to see whether it really is inhibiting) should be changed. There is no dogma of CAD/CAM organizational form.

3.6 General Influences on the Organization of CAD/CAM

Technology changes faster than people's behavior. The attempt to change the organization to meet changes in technology generally takes place before the majority of people are ready for it. Thus, while the process of organizational change is going on, a parallel process of preparing people to accept this change is necessary. Initially, this means that people have to be given some understanding of what CAD/CAM is and what it can do. Many of them will be afraid of change and may do everything possible to prevent it. To overcome this fear, management must build a company culture of communication, consensus, and trust.

In many ways, the introduction of new technologies is as painful for traditional "management" as it is for traditional "employees." The employee sees change going on, and often expects to be a loser from such changes through losing employment, losing power over an "empire" of underlings, losing power by having to share information, or having to accept a broader job description with the consequent risk of having to carry out mundane or unpleasant tasks. Management, however, sees a big risk in investing large sums of money in new technologies such as CAD/CAM (maybe it won't work). Training is required on a large scale (we pay people to work, not to attend courses), and then there is the danger that highly trained people will leave the company (we wasted all that money training them).

Work will be carried out more quickly with CAD/CAM. Decisions will have to be made faster. The need for accurate project planning and control will increase. Management will become more complex. It will no longer be a case of having a set of job descriptions and a set of employees who could be told, through a chain of several middle managers, to do this job and that job. Instead, managers will be required to put together people and sets of people to carry out specific tasks. Management may have to help employees achieve requirements, rather than just ordering them to do it and employing vast numbers of supervisors and group leaders to clean up the mess.

The reward system of the organization will have to be modified so that it supports those who support the introduction of new technologies. It is as if the scale of new technology investment is such that a new form of partnership is required between management and staff. Such a partnership can be looked at from either side and seen to have advantages and disadvantages. The challenge, however, is not to look inside the company to see who is the "winner," since the real winner will be the company that looks outward to meet customer requirements and consequently attains its objectives.

3.7 The Implications of CAD/CAM for Different Parts of the Company

CAD/CAM affects most departments in a company, not just those where the system is actually in use. The most obvious impact will be in the design engineering and manufacturing engineering departments, but production, purchasing, sales, and personnel will also be affected. It is therefore in the interests of the business that directors and senior managers from all departments understand and are committed to the implementation of a CAD/CAM system.

3.8 Implications at Corporate Level

The main reasons given for implementing a CAD/CAM system are improved quality, shortened lead times, and reduced costs. Within those broad categories can be fitted most of the detailed justifications given in CAD/CAM projects. However, the most commonly expressed feeling of directors and senior managers after installing a CAD/CAM system is a sense of having moved the company into the so-called high-tech era. Certainly, the company may experience a marked improvement in its perceived image in the marketplace. However, this feeling of making real progress in the world of high technology is only the starting point from which the real work must begin.

If the implementation has been thoroughly planned, many of the implications for the organization will have been discussed and evaluated and an implementation plan put into operation. Sadly, this is very rarely the case. The company is often only at the beginning of the real work of putting the system to best use and ensuring that all the benefits stated in the project plan and confirmed by the vendor are realized.

The greatest overall change in the organization should come from the improved cooperation between engineering and manufacturing activities. This is true even if the organization only has CAD and not CAM, but it is especially true if both CAD and CAM systems are installed, since the CAD system is not there just to produce more drawings faster than the previous manual methods. It is there to define the product to be manufactured in as complete a way as possible after taking into account all the factors involved in its manufacture. The CAD system is therefore defining a product which, when manufactured, will operate efficiently and reliably, and be cost-effective to make, in terms of both the manufacturing facilities and raw materials required for its production.

3.9 Implications for the Divisional Organization

In much of the manufacturing industry it has traditionally been part of company policy for divisions to compete with each other for investment, human resources, and profitability. Such policies have given rise to the resource-consuming debate over who pays for engineering changes. Put more simply: Whose fault was it? Who's to blame? The installation of a CAD/CAM system can have a profound effect on that debate in as much as the question of fault or blame does not arise. This is because the design is developed in conjunction with manufacturing from the concept stage. Therefore the responsibility for the design and manufacture of the product is shared by all parties. A more fundamental benefit of the new way of working is that the number of changes is greatly reduced; thus many of the problems associated with traditional methods will no longer occur. This can have a dramatic effect on reducing product cost and lead times.

In the traditional environment, designers and engineers very rarely communicate with the production and industrial engineers and have little knowledge of what they actually do with a particular design. CAD/CAM offers both groups of engineers the opportunity and the means to understand each other's point of view and at the same time produce a better quality product in a shorter time at a reduced cost.

Once this type of working has been introduced and accepted it will not be difficult to set up multidisciplinary teams of engineers who are responsible for the process from concept design to production. These teams may be formed for the duration of the project or may be product-oriented and operate as a team on many projects. It may be that the introduction of CAD/CAM will lead to the reemergence of the "engineer" who is responsible for all aspects of the product from concept design to manufacture. The implications for divisional organizations are considerable. At the very least, they will need to cooperate and work together as opposed to working against each other. At the very best, the divisional boundaries will disappear.

Implications for the design department

Apart from the normal benefits associated with CAD/CAM (such as improved quality of design and the ability to try more options more quickly), there is one major change that will affect the design department. That change is associated with increased involvement of engineering and manufacturing at the concept design stage. The design department will become more integrated into the business of the company and will more readily recognize the value of discussing concepts and ideas with other departments downstream of its own activity.

Implications for the drafting department

In many cases the first department to install a CAD/CAM system has been the drafting department. This has often occurred because CAD/CAM was installed as an electronic drawing board to produce more drawings faster. In a fully integrated environment the drafting department may be the first department to disappear. As the functional differences among designer, engineer, drafter, and manufacturing engineer begin to fade, so the need for a drafting department recedes. In the meantime, however, the drafting department becomes the focus of attention both for those who are interested in the success of CAD/CAM and for those who hope it will fail.

For people working in the drafting department there is the question of who should work on the CAD/CAM system and who should continue at the drawing board. Managers should avoid creating an elitist group of CAD/CAM users who work in a separate area (or even a completely separate room) from their colleagues.

Implications for the manufacturing engineering department

For this group of engineers the implementation of a CAD/CAM system appears as a recognition of their importance to the manufacturing process and as an opportunity to help engineering avoid those mistakes which must be fixed at a later date. Their role in the design and manufacturing process is elevated from being a passive receiver of design engineering's attempt to define product information to being an active participant in the design and creation of the final product. Any company not making the most of this opportunity should seriously question their CAD/CAM objectives. The manufacturing engineering department may eventually be grouped with design and engineering into a single product development department.

Implications for the EDP department

In a CAD/CAM environment the role of the EDP department changes from one of provider of computing resources to a provider of support and guidance. Once the overall CAD/CAM strategy has been defined, the EDP department may help in setting the systems strategy and standards for equipment. It may also act as an adviser when system upgrades take place and may undertake some engineering applications programming.

In traditional organizations, the EDP department is generally closely associated with finance and administration, and manages the company's computing applications such as payroll, accounting, office automation, and sales. CAD/CAM is primarily an engineering resource, and should be managed by the engineering departments rather than by finance and administration. The EDP department may know a lot about bits and bytes, but very little about CAD/CAM and engineering. The engineering computing function should be allowed to develop without undue interference from the EDP department. Once CAD/CAM and EDP are of similar importance to the company and are reporting to the highest levels of functional departmental management, it may be time for them to merge (with a title such as information department). By this time, their importance will be such that the manager of this function will report directly to the CEO.

Implications for the marketing department

This department will be extremely interested in any technique that can reduce the time and cost of getting a product to market. A reduction in production costs will be appreciated, as will the flexibility that comes from the ease of making minor product modifications. The marketing department should also benefit from a variety of secondary effects, such as an improvement in the company's image and improvements in communicating product information through advertising and directly to potential clients. The other major implication for the marketing department is that it will probably have to generate more sales to help pay for the CAD/CAM system.

Implications for the production department

Although CAD/CAM appears to be an engineering-oriented activity, it can have major effects outside the engineering department. One area that can be a major beneficiary of the introduction of CAD/CAM is the production department. After all, the engineering departments define the product and process information so that the product can be manufactured by the production department. Many of the problems that occur on the shop floor result from the reception of incomplete or incorrect information. In the CAD/CAM environment, once the product and process information has been defined in the engineering database, there is no reason why the production department should not directly access this data and view it in exactly the same state that it is seen by engineers.

Chapter 4

CAD/CAM and Finance

4.1 The Need for Financial Appraisal of the CAD/CAM Plan

Each year companies will invest in a variety of new long-term capital projects. Potential projects will cover a range of activities such as the introduction of new products, improvement of the distribution network, an increase in the number of sales outlets, improvements in manufacturing efficiency, development of the corporate image, improvement of working conditions, and implementation of CAD/CAM. Although the potential projects cover a variety of areas and have a variety of short-term objectives, their ultimate aim is the same: to help to meet customer requirements.

Top management must make a selection of the most "profitable" projects from those presented. Perhaps a group of projects giving a mixture of short-term and long-term results would be most suitable. The task of selection is a critical one, since many of the proposed projects will involve a large initial investment, have a major effect on the company in the long term, not be easily stopped once started, or call for major upheavals in the company. Management's approval of a given project will partly be based on its own knowledge of long-term company objectives. It will, however, also need to have a detailed description and justification of the costs and benefits of each potential project, which requires input from a variety of sources such as marketing, engineering, manufacturing, personnel, and finance. This chapter describes some of the financial information that the CAD/CAM manager will need from departmental sources when proposing a major investment in CAD/CAM.

The justification should show the required capital and running costs associated with the project, the expected benefits, the expected return, the risk associated with the investment, and the effect of the investment on other areas of the company. Without such a justification, top management will not be able to choose the most suitable areas to invest in or to know how much capital should be made available.

The selection of capital projects is an activity that top management is faced with year after year. The CAD/CAM manager may see the CAD/CAM project as being of prime importance; yet to top management it is just one of many projects to be appraised. A poorly presented and incomplete proposal from the CAD/CAM manager will probably result in management having a very poor view of both CAD/CAM and the CAD/CAM manager. The CAD/CAM manager should also realize that even if the project looks profitable in the justification, it will not automatically be accepted. Management is aware that many projects which have appeared profitable on paper have led to major losses because of unforeseen or changing circumstances. A profitable project may also be rejected because it is less profitable than other projects being proposed or perhaps because it does not fit into the overall corporate plan.

4.2 Some Important Concepts in Financial Appraisal

Depreciation

When accountants prepare a company's profit and loss statement, they use a technique known as "matching." Generally, it is relatively easy to identify sales made during a year. Then costs incurred during the year should be matched against these sales. This is not always easy, as the following example shows.

If an expensive machine has been bought during the year and is expected to be used over 5 years, then it would not be correct accounting practice to include the total cost of the machine in 1 year's profit and loss figures, with nothing included in the following years. Correct practice would be to match some fraction of the machine's cost (known as *depreciation*) against sales in each of the 5 years. Thus depreciation is a symbolic, annual, noncash charge representing the gradual recovery over a project's lifetime of the capital invested in it.

The amount of an investment that can be depreciated and the period of depreciation are laid down by government regulations. Various methods of depreciation are allowed, but once a company has chosen a particular method it is expected to retain it for consistency in the presentation of its results.

With the most simple method of depreciation—called the *straight-line method*—the amount of depreciation is constant for each year. Thus a $1 million machine depreciated over 5 years would result in a "cost" of $200,000 being included in the profit and loss account in each of the 5 years.

Under the *sum-of-the-years* method of depreciation, the annual depreciation is a variable fraction of the original investment. The fraction is the number of remaining years divided by the sum of the years. Thus for a 4-year project the sum is (4 + 3 + 2 + 1), i.e., 10, and the first-year depreciation rate is 4/10, i.e., 40 percent.

Under the *double-declining balance* method of depreciation, the annual depreciation is again variable and twice that which would apply if the straight-line method were applied to the undepreciated balance in that year. For 5-year depreciation of an initial investment of \$100,000, the first year's depreciation under the double-declining method would be \$40,000 (i.e., 2 × \$100,000/5). The undepreciated balance is then \$60,000, so the second-year depreciation is \$24,000 (i.e., 2 × \$60,000/5). The undepreciated balance is then \$36,000, so the third-year depreciation is \$14,400 (i.e., 2 × \$36,000/5). The double-declining method can be illustrated by a post-1987 U.S. tax reform example. Although the CAD/CAM system is depreciated over 5 years, only half a year of depreciation is allowed for the first year (and consequently for the sixth year). The annual depreciation allowed would be 20 percent in year 1, 32 percent in year 2, 19.20 percent in year 3, 11.52 percent in year 4, and so on.

When assets such as machine tools and computer-based systems (such as CAD/CAM systems) are being depreciated they are often described as being carried "at book value." Depreciation is sometimes said to be a "book value," since it appears in the company's books of account; yet from another point of view (called a *cash view*), it does not even exist. From a cash view, when the company buys the machine, it pays \$1 million in cash immediately; no further cash is paid over the following years.

Net income

A glance at the financial statements of a company will show the term *net income*, which is the result (roughly speaking) of subtracting the cost of sales, depreciation, tax, and other expenses from the annual sales. Since the calculation of net income involves subtracting depreciation from net sales, net income is another book value. Book values are of limited help in appraising the investment in a project because they do not take into account the timing of cash items associated with the investment. For example, in the case described above, the company has to pay out over \$1 million in cash when buying the machine. It does not pay out \$200,000 in each of 5 years.

Cash flow

The incremental cash inflows resulting from investing in a project come in the form of sales revenues, tax credits, and so on. The incremental cash outflows are due to payments for labor, equipment and sundries, operating expenses, taxes, and so on.

The difference between the total cash inflows resulting from the project and the total cash outflows is called the *cash flow* of the project. A positive cash flow for a project indicates that over its lifetime, cash inflows resulting from the investment will exceed cash outflows.

In the long term, a company's survival depends on its being profitable. In the short term, this is not enough. The company also needs to have cash to pay bills for items such as salaries and telephone calls. Financial analyses generally look at the effect of the project on a company's cash or working capital. (Working capital refers to anything which can be converted into cash at short notice. Apart from cash, it includes accounts receivable, stock, accounts payable, and other items realizable within a year).

Time value of cash flows

Which has more value—$1000 received today, $1000 received in a year, or $1000 received in 5 years? Assume that the $1000 can be invested at a fixed 10 percent annual interest rate, then

$1000 received	Worth in 5 years
Today	$1610.51
In 1 year	$1464.10
In 5 years	$1000

Thus $1000 received today will be worth more than $1000 received in the future.

The calculations can be carried out backward, starting from known future values and calculating the equivalent present values. Again, assume a constant 10 percent annual interest rate.

$200,000 received	Present value
In 5 years	$124,184
In 4 years	136,603
In 3 years	150,263
In 2 years	165,289
In 1 year	181,818
Today	200,000

This technique of working backward to find the value of money at a particular time when its value at another time is known is called *discounting*. It is an important concept in investment analysis and highlights the importance of the timing of cash inflows and cash outflows.

Timing in cash flow calculations

The initial investment in a project is assumed to take place in year 0. Consequent cash flows of a 5-year project occur in year 1, year 2, year 3, year 4, and year 5.

Depreciation—again

It has been seen that depreciation is a book value item and not a cash flow item (the cash has flown at investment time) and should not therefore be included in a cash flow calculation. This is not to say that depreciation has no effect on the overall cash flow calculation. Since depreciation is subtracted from net sales before the tax contribution is calculated, it affects the income tax paid. Income tax is a very real cash outflow; thus depreciation, by reducing the income tax outflow, has an effect on the overall cash flow.

Before tax or after tax?

Investment appraisals are usually carried out on an after-tax basis. Income tax is clearly a cash flow item. Investment credits and grants associated with the project will also create cash flows of some sort. As their timing may not be spread evenly over the lifetime of the project, it is logical to take their effect into account by considering the after-tax situation.

Present value of cash flows

The relative value of two investments which occur at different times is not immediately clear. To clarify the position, all cash flows for each project are discounted back to the present. To calculate the present value of cash inflows arising during a 5-year project, an expected interest rate for the investment in the project must first be decided by the company. This rate will then be used to discount the cash flows. For example, the company may decide that the investment should generate a rate of return of 20 percent per year.

If the expected annual cash inflows received at year end are

Year 1	Year 2	Year 3	Year 4	Year 5	Total
$110,000	$130,000	$160,000	$220,000	$280,000	$900,000

then their present value is calculated by discounting them at a 20 percent rate. This gives

Year 1	Year 2	Year 3	Year 4	Year 5	Total
$91,666	$90,278	$92,593	$106,096	$112,526	$493,159

The present value of the cash inflows is therefore seen to be $493,159 (and not $900,000). The concepts introduced here apply to investments in all types of projects. For a CAD/CAM project it is particularly important to understand the origins of the various cash inflows and outflows.

4.3 The Productivity Ratio Trap

The terms *productivity ratio* and *productivity* have many definitions. They are often used to express in some way the ratio between the result of an activity and the effort put into that activity (i.e., the ratio of output to input).

However, the definitions of these terms are so vague that they have taken on all sorts of meanings. For example, some people define the productivity of a CAD/CAM system as the number of drawings produced in a given number of work-hours with the CAD/CAM system divided by the number produced in the same time period without the system. This is an unusual definition of the term productivity ratio as it only considers the ratio of two output quantities without taking into account the change in input effort. Obviously, the input effort should also be considered since it has been increased by the purchase and implementation of the CAD/CAM system.

Since the definitions of productivity ratio and productivity are so vague, the CAD/CAM manager must not fall into the trap of misinterpreting values quoted for them. Even for a particular system, the ratio will depend on many things, for example, the application for which the system is being used and the experience of the people using the system.

The more factors that are considered, the more difficult it becomes to attach any real meaning to the term productivity ratio. Consider the case of an application that required 100 hours of work by a skilled craftsman, a CAD/CAM system that has a productivity ratio of 5:1 for this type of application, and another CAD/CAM system that has a productivity ratio of 2:1. If the first system can only be handled by a specialist who has used it for 3 years, whereas the second can be used by anyone after 2 weeks of training, which system is more suitable? Or assume that the first system can only be used for 4 hours of work on the application, whereas the second can be used for 10 hours. Which system is more suitable? What does productivity ratio really mean for these systems? If it refers to time, what conclusion would one draw if it turned out that the first system costs 5 times as much as the second?

If it refers to cost, is the cost considered the sum of the cost of the system per hour and the direct labor cost per hour, or has the cost of training and installation also to be taken into account? There is a real danger that the potential savings resulting from use of the system will be evaluated incorrectly if only raw productivity ratios are used.

Consider another example. Assume that a four-person drawing office currently produces 300 drawings per week. Each person is paid $600 per week, i.e., a total salary bill of $2400. The drawing office decides to invest in a CAD/CAM system with a promised productivity ratio of 2:1 (i.e., each person can then produce 150 drawings per week). Since two people at a salary cost of $1200 can now produce 300 drawings per week, there is an apparent saving of $1200 per week. However, this saving will not be made while the two other people are still employed by the company in the drawing office. Since the total salary cost is still $2400 per week, to which must be added the extra overhead resulting from use of the CAD/CAM system, there is actually no saving at all but a loss.

It may well be that savings would actually occur in the above case, but that could only happen as a result of further action, e.g., if the two people were laid off or assigned to productive work in another part of the company, or if they were kept in the drawing office but to do something that would decrease costs associated with, for example, scrap or rework. An alternative would be that their work with the system results in increased turnover for the company. This implies, however, that the use of CAD/CAM would no longer solely be intended to reduce costs but also to increase revenues. This subject is discussed in more detail below; however, before leaving this section, it must be stressed that great care must be taken when interpreting productivity ratios and using them to calculate potential cost reductions and revenue increases.

4.4 Determining Project Costs

When investigating investment in CAD/CAM, managers should include among their major tasks the identification of the expected costs and revenues, and an estimation of their timing. Since major benefits are unlikely to arise in the short term, the investigation should at least cover the intermediate term. As such systems are often depreciated over 5 years, this may well be a suitable time period to examine. The major costs include the following.

In year 0

- Initial investment in hardware and software
- Initial training and education
- Shipping and installation costs

- Cost of selecting the system

In years 1 to 5

- Further purchases of hardware and software
- System maintenance and insurance
- Further training and education
- System management and operations
- Development of symbol and part libraries
- Interfaces to other systems
- Development of new procedures
- Modifications to existing procedures
- Purchases of sundry supplies and accessories
- Costs involved in attending user group meetings
- Income tax resulting from the extra profit generated by the project (note that income tax is paid during the year after it is incurred and that while the project is losing money, it is effectively reducing company profits and therefore decreasing the amount of tax to be paid).

The total costs that might be incurred by the project over 5 years (on a nondiscounted basis) are shown in Table 4.1.

Among the major lessons to be drawn from the figures in Table 4.1 (which are fictional but realistic) are (1) that the initial system purchase, which often appears frighteningly high to potential buyers, actually represents a fairly small part of total expenditure, and (2) that

TABLE 4.1 Total Costs Incurred by Project over 5 Years (on a nondiscounted basis)

Initial system purchase	$ 500,000
Further hardware and software purchase	400,000
Shipping, site preparation, and installation	20,000
Maintenance and insurance	500,000
Training and education	300,000
Procedure development	50,000
Running costs	400,000
System selection	90,000
Library development costs	50,000
Modification costs	50,000
Supplies and accessories	40,000
Travel and meetings	100,000
Total	$2,500,000

over 5 years, training costs, running costs, and maintenance costs are about the same as system purchase costs.

It is unlikely that figures of the type shown above (i.e., undiscounted and with no indication of cash flow timings) will be sufficient for investment appraisal. It is more likely that a discounted cash flow approach will be required.

As a first step, the annual cash outflows should be estimated as shown in Table 4.2. Then these cash outflows should be discounted at the accepted company rate, e.g., 20 percent. This would give

Year 0	Year 1	Year 2	Year 3	Year 4	Year 5
$700,000	$251,667	$236,458	$218,171	$200,858	$142,265

TABLE 4.2 Annual Cash Outflows

In Year 0	
System selection	$ 90,000
Hardware and software	500,000
Training and education	100,000
Shipping and installation	10,000
Total	$700,000
In Year 1	
Hardware and software	$100,000
Shipping, site preparation, and installation	2,000
Maintenance and insurance	70,000
Training and education	40,000
Management and operations	40,000
Library development	15,000
Interfaces	6,000
Procedure development	15,000
Supplies and accessories	4,000
Travel and meetings	10,000
Total	$302,000
In Year 2	
Hardware and software	$100,000
Shipping and installation	4,000
Maintenance and insurance	87,500
Training and education	40,000
Management and operations	60,000
Library development	5,000
Interfaces	8,000
Procedure development	15,000
Supplies and accessories	6,000
Travel and meetings	15,000
Total	$340,500

TABLE 4.2 Annual Cash Outflows (*Continued*)

In Year 3	
Hardware and software	$100,000
Shipping and installation	2,000
Maintenance and insurance	100,000
Training and education	40,000
Management and operations	80,000
Library development	5,000
Interfaces	10,000
Procedure development	12,000
Supplies and accessories	8,000
Travel and meetings	20,000
Total	$377,000
In Year 4	
Hardware and software	$100,000
Shipping and installation	2,000
Maintenance and insurance	112,500
Training and education	40,000
Management and operations	100,000
Library development	5,000
Interfaces	12,000
Procedure development	10,000
Supplies and accessories	10,000
Travel and meetings	25,000
Total	$416,500
In Year 5	
Maintenance and insurance	$125,000
Training and education	40,000
Management and operations	120,000
Library development	5,000
Interfaces	14,000
Procedure development	8,000
Supplies and accessories	12,000
Travel and meetings	30,000
Total	$354,000

4.5 Forecasting Revenues

It is often more difficult to estimate the financial benefits of CAD/CAM than to estimate its cost. The benefits can manifest themselves in various ways, such as a reduction in cost, an increase in revenue, or no lost revenue.

Referring back to the example of the four-person drawing office described earlier, these three possibilities can be illustrated as follows. If two people are laid off, then salary costs can be reduced. If all four people are retained, their increased output could result in increased turnover. However, in a particularly competitive market, it may be necessary to retain all four people just to maintain revenue. Another way to reduce costs could be to retain all four people, maintain the same output, but increase the quality of the output—in this case engineering drawings. This could lead to cost savings at production time, either through reduced rework or reduced scrap.

It can be seen that even before attempting to quantify the benefits of using CAD/CAM, it is necessary to identify where they come from. The following classification is used in the program PEARS.

1. Cost of sales
   a. Reduction in number of designers; drafters; supervisors; checkers; technical, administrative, and clerical staffs; model makers; process planners; and part programmers
   b. Reduction in materials through optimized design, better documentation, reduced scrap and rework, reduced erroneous order and manufacture of parts, and standardized tooling
   c. Reduction in energy consumption through optimized design
   d. Reduction in work to be subcontracted
   e. Reduction of production overhead, e.g., through production of larger, standardized batches
   f. Reduction of stocks and work in progress, e.g., through standardization and reduced lead times
2. Other manufacturing costs
   a. Reduction in cost of holding goods for sale through reduced stocks
   b. Reduction in cost of holding goods through improved space utilization
3. Revenues
   a. Increase in revenues resulting from shorter delivery times (produce quicker, then sell quicker; produce new product range quicker, so earlier launch and higher initial sales are possible)
   b. Increase in revenues resulting from more reliable delivery dates
   c. Increase in revenues resulting from ability to produce to exact customer specifications
   d. Increase in revenues resulting from better quotations resulting in more orders
   e. Increase in revenues resulting from more reliable quotations, thus reducing unexpected costs
   f. Increase in revenues resulting from higher quality products
   g. Increase in revenues resulting from lower prices for same goods
   h. Increase in revenues resulting from sale of CAD/CAM services

To quantify such gains, management should involve people from many parts of the company, discuss the estimated figures in detail and, if necessary, have them analyzed by an independent expert. For example, to find out what effect CAD/CAM will have on proposals and revenues, marketing and sales personnel must be consulted. Information from other companies may be of use. The major gains should be investigated in detail.

The aim is to produce a table of quantified benefits in the form shown in Table 4.3. These values will then be discounted at the same rate as the costs, i.e., 20 percent, and a table of discounted benefits drawn up (Table 4.4). It will then be possible to compare the costs and benefits and to quantify the return on the investment.

TABLE 4.3 Benefits of CAD/CAM (in dollars)

	Year 1	Year 2	Year 3	Year 4	Year 5
Reduction in cost of sales	160,000	200,000	240,000	280,000	320,000
Reduction in other manufacturing costs		80,000	160,000	240,000	320,000
Increase in revenues	200,000	400,000	1,000,000	1,400,000	2,000,000

TABLE 4.4 Discounted Benefits of CAD/CAM (in dollars)

	Year 1	Year 2	Year 3	Year 4	Year 5
Reduction in cost of sales	133,333	138,888	138,888	135,031	128,601
Reduction in other manufacturing costs		55,555	92,593	115,741	128,601
Increase in revenues	166,666	277,777	578,704	675,154	803,755
Annual benefit	300,000	472,222	810,185	925,926	1,060,957

4.6 Methods Used to Evaluate Projects

Various methods are used for calculating the return from an investment. They vary in origin, complexity, and usefulness. Four frequently used methods are described here.

Accounting rate of return (ARR)

The *accounting rate of return* (ARR) is a classical accountant's calculation in which depreciation appears. This implies that it is more like the calculation involved in preparing a company's profit and loss statement, than a calculation of cash flow. The ARR is the ratio of the accounting income generated by the project to the total investment expressed as a percentage.

Payback time

Payback time is the time required for a project's revenues to equal the initial cash outlay.

Investment	\$1,000,000
Annual revenue	\$400,000
Payback time	$\frac{1{,}000{,}000}{400{,}000} = 2\frac{1}{2}$ years

ARR and payback are "quick and dirty" calculations and do not generally take account of the time value of money. In addition, the payback method ignores the effect of revenues occurring after the payback period. These revenues may have a significant effect. Discounted cash flow methods are usually more suitable for assessing the expected profit from an individual project in financial terms .

Net present value (NPV)

The present value of cash inflows and outflows was discussed previously. The *net present value* of a project at any given time is calculated by subtracting from the investment the sum of the discounted cash flows up to that time.

$$\text{NPV} = -I + \sum_{t=1,n} \frac{(R_t - C_t)}{(1+DR)^t}$$

where I = investment in year 0
DR = discount rate
R_t = revenue in year t
C_t = costs in year t
n = project lifetime in years

As an example

Investment	\$1000
Discount rate	20 percent
Project lifetime	2 years
Cash inflow in year 1	\$850
Cash outflow in year 1	\$250
Discounted cash flow in year 1	\$500
Cash inflow in year 2	\$1050
Cash outflow in year 2	\$300
Discounted cash flow in year 2	\$520.83
NPV	−1000 + 500 + 520.83 = \$20.83

In this case the net present value of the investment (which was expected to earn 20 percent) is positive, i.e., it is earning more than 20 percent. (If the NPV turns out to be negative, this means that the discounted cash flows are less than the initial investment, i.e., the project is not making money at the required rate.)

Discounted cash flow return on investment (ROI)

The net present value method of evaluating an investment is easy to understand. However, it requires prior selection of an acceptable rate of return. An alternative method, known as *internal rate of return on investment*, calculates the rate of return that corresponds to the net present value of the project being equal to zero (i.e., investment is exactly equal to the sum of the discounted cash flows).

The rate of return is calculated from the NPV formula.

$$\mathrm{NPV} = -I + \sum_{t=1,n} \frac{(R_t - C_t)}{(1 + \mathrm{DR})^t}$$

with NPV = 0,

$$I = \sum_{t=1,n} \frac{(R_t - C_t)}{(1 + \mathrm{DR})^t}$$

Using the same figures as given in the net present value example,

$$1000 = \frac{600}{1 + \mathrm{DR}} + \frac{750}{(1 + \mathrm{DR})^2}$$

so DR = 21.6 percent, i.e., the yield of this project is 21.6 percent.

4.7 Sensitivity and Risk Analysis

Even when the rate of return for a project has been calculated, questions of the type "but what if...?" still arise. Sensitivity analysis and risk analysis try to answer these questions. Sensitivity analysis can be used to look at each cash flow item individually and answer the question "What is the effect on the overall rate of return if all other items have been correctly estimated but this particular one miscalculated by x percent?" Each item can be checked in this way, and generally it is found that there are a few items that have much more effect on the rate of return than the others. For example, a 20 percent variation in one item may lead to a 1 percent change in the rate of return, whereas the same variation in another item may lead to a 5 percent change.

Risk analysis is carried out to estimate the probability that the rate of return will be met. One way of doing this is to assign probabilities to expected values for each cash flow item. Thus, instead of assuming that the value for operating costs will be $10,000, it could be decided that there is a 5 percent probability that it will be $8000, 10 percent that it will be $9000, 70 percent that it will be $10,000, 10 percent that it will be $11,000, and 5 percent that it will be $12,000. Similar probabilities could be calculated for the other items. The rate of return calculations would then be calculated as a function of these probabilities. The result would show the range of values for the rate of return and their associated probabilities. It should not be forgotten that these calculations always use estimates, and consequently there is some uncertainty. Sensitivity analysis identifies the items that critically affect calculations. Risk analysis provides a range of possible values for the outcome, rather than a single value.

4.8 The Request for Funding

The request for funding has to be intelligible to engineers, accountants, and top management. It must therefore follow the company's usual capital budgeting procedures, go through the usual administrative steps, and be accompanied by the usual paperwork.

The request for funding document will probably contain a brief overview of the CAD/CAM project and a summary of its costs, revenues, and benefits. It must also show when funds will be committed. The request for funding has to be accepted at several levels of the hierarchy. At some levels, the form of the request becomes as important as its content. Once the project has been accepted and is under way, the CAD/CAM manager will have to report periodically on the progress of the project, expenditures actually incurred, and revenues generated. If costs rise faster than expected, it may be necessary to make a further request.

4.9 Recovering the Costs of CAD/CAM

At the company level, the costs of CAD/CAM can only be recovered through an increase in turnover or a decrease in operating costs. Within the company, though, there are various ways of recovering the costs of CAD/CAM. Some companies will regard CAD/CAM as an overhead to be carried at the company level, others will carry it at the manufacturing department level, the engineering department level, or the design department level. Some companies will charge CAD/CAM to projects at a fixed rate; others will charge CAD/CAM to projects as a function of the CAD/CAM resources used by that project. In the latter case, the calculation may be simply a function of the workstation hours used by the project, or it may be more complex and also include CPU usage, disk space used, and so on.

Some companies charge CAD/CAM out at a recovery rate per workstation-hour that results from dividing the total cost of CAD/CAM over 5 years by the total number of expected workstation-hours in that period. As an example, if a four-workstation system is used 7 hours per day for 220 days per year over 5 years then a total of 30,800 (4 × 7 × 220 × 5) workstation-hours will be available. If the total cost of CAD/CAM over 5 years is $650,000, then a recovery rate of $650,000/30,800, i.e., $21.10 per workstation-hour, could be charged.

The way in which a company recovers its CAD/CAM costs will depend on its CAD/CAM objectives—there is no "best" way. Two things should be kept in mind though. Firstly, CAD/CAM can be expensive. If, immediately after installation (when productivity will probably decrease), projects are billed at the full recovery rate of CAD/CAM, then project managers will avoid using it. This will lead to a vicious circle, with the recovery rate rising as an attempt is made to recover costs from a reduced number of workstation-hours and the number of users decreasing further because of the rising cost. Secondly, the recovery rate as described depends on the number of hours that the workstations are in use. Introduction of a second shift would double the number of hours in use and significantly reduce the recovery rate. (This is the classical justification for shift work when expensive equipment is being used.)

4.10 Leasing—An Alternative to Purchase

In the same way that a financial model can be built up to evaluate purchase of a CAD/CAM system, it is also possible to build models to evaluate leasing a system and to compare leasing to purchasing. The basic philosophy of these models is similar to the purchase model in that present values are used. There are three differences in the calculation. Firstly, since the monthly lease payments can be expensed, tax savings will occur. Secondly, leasing avoids the major up-front cash flow due to purchasing. Thirdly, the tax savings resulting from depreciation are lost when leasing.

$$\text{NPV} = -\sum_{c=1,m} \frac{L_c}{(1+\text{MDR})^c} + \sum_{t=1,n} \frac{(R_t - C_t)}{(1+\text{ADR})^t}$$

where ADR = annual discount rate
MDR = monthly discount rate
R_t = revenue in year t
C_t = costs in year t
n = project lifetime in years
L_C = monthly lease payment
m = project lifetime in months

For a given set of values, the company can then determine whether it is preferable to purchase or lease.

4.11 An Example of Financial Appraisal

The following example shows typical costs and benefits associated with CAD/CAM investment. The output shown (from the program PEARS) gives details of the financial characteristics of the CAD/CAM project and of its total effect on the company's financial situation. The program, which can be used by both engineers and accountants, correctly carries out the tedious and complex number-crunching associated with financial justification of this sort. Costing about the same as 1 day of an engineer's time, it can analyze very quickly many different scenarios of CAD/CAM investment and use that would otherwise require days or weeks of effort. Managers, engineers, and accountants are freed from the mechanical side of the calculations and can concentrate on selecting the CAD/CAM solution that will most closely meet the company's objectives. Tables 4.5 and 4.6 show the 5-year statement of earnings and flow of funds in the absence of the CAD/CAM project. Table 4.7 shows the estimated costs and benefits of CAD/CAM translated into their effect on sales and expenses. Tables 4.8 and 4.9 show the 5-year statement of earnings and flow of funds that will result from the introduction of CAD/CAM.

To emphasize the change in the movement of retained cash, the following two tables would be prepared. Table 4.10 shows a comparison of the equity value of the company (i.e., the total of share capital and retained earnings) with and without the project. Table 4.11 shows the cash generated for the company with and without the project.

TABLE 4.5 Five-Year Statement of Earnings in Absence of CAD/CAM Project
(in thousands of dollars)

	Year 0	Year 1	Year 2	Year 3	Year 4	Year 5
Sales	20,000	20,000	20,000	20,000	20,000	20,000
Cost of sales (direct)	(11,046.5)	(11,046.5)	(11,046.5)	(11,046.5)	(11,046.5)	(11,046.5)
Cost of sales (indirect)	(1,050.5)	(1,050.5)	(1,050.5)	(1,050.5)	(1,050.5)	(1,050.5)
	7,903	7,903	7,903	7,903	7,903	7,903
Sales expenses	(1,950)	(1,950)	(1,950)	(1,950)	(1,950)	(1,950)
G&A	(2,980)	(2,980)	(2,980)	(2,980)	(2,980)	(2,980)
R&D	(810)	(810)	(810)	(810)	(810)	(810)
	2,163	2,163	2,163	2,163	2,163	2,163
Other income	(350)	(350)	(350)	(350)	(350)	(350)
Other expenses	(235)	(235)	(235)	(235)	(235)	(235)
Interest expense	(225)	(225)	(191)	(150)	(100)	(50)
	2,053	2,053	2,087	2,128	2,178	2,228
Taxation	(821.2)	(821.2)	(834.8)	(851.2)	(871.2)	(891.2)
	1,231.8	1,231.8	1,252.2	1,276.8	1,306.8	1,336.8
Proposed dividend	0	(200)	(300)	(300)	(300)	(400)
	1,231.8	1,031.8	1,052.2	976.8	1,006.8	936.8
Prior retained earnings	19,153	20,384.8	21,416.6	22,468.8	23,445.6	24,452.4
Current retained earnings	20,384.8	21,416.6	22,468.8	23,445.6	24,452.4	25,389.2

TABLE 4.6 Five-Year Flow of Funds in Absence of CAD/CAM Project
(in thousands of dollars)

	Year 1	Year 2	Year 3	Year 4	Year 5
Profit before taxation	2053	2087	2128	2178	2228
Depreciation	1780	1780	1580	1180	1180
Total funds	3833	3867	3708	3358	3408
Dividend paid	(0)	(200)	(200)	(300)	(300)
Fixed asset investment	(0)	(0)	(0)	(0)	(0)
Taxation paid	(821.2)	(821.2)	(834.8)	(851.2)	(871.2)
Repayment of long-term debt	(680)	(820)	(1000)	(1000)	(1000)
Increase in working capital	2331.8	2025.8	1673.2	1206.8	1236.8
Movement in bank and cash	2331.8	2025.8	1673.2	1206.8	1236.8

TABLE 4.7 Estimated Effect of CAD/CAM Project
(in thousands of dollars)

	Year 0	Year 1	Year 2	Year 3	Year 4	Year 5
Sales and Expenses						
Increase in sales		200	400	1000	1400	2000
Decrease in COS (direct)		160	200	240	280	320
Decrease in sales expenses			80	160	240	320
Decrease in G&A		(140.4)	(161.2)	(181.6)	(202)	(202)
Decrease in COS (indirect)		219	518.8	1218.4	1718	2438
CAD/CAM Project Investment Costs						
Fixed assets	600	102	104	102	102	0
Cost of sales (indirect)	100	164	208.5	248	287.5	327
R&D		36	28	27	27	27
Total	700	302	340.5	377.5	417.5	354

TABLE 4.8 Five-Year Statement of Earnings Including Estimated Changes in Sales and Expenses Resulting from CAD/CAM Project
(in thousands of dollars)

	Year 0	Year 1	Year 2	Year 3	Year 4	Year 5
Sales	20,000	20,200	20,400	21,000	21,400	22,000
Cost of sales (direct)	(11,046.5)	(10,886.5)	(10,846.5)	(10,806.5)	(10,766.5)	(10,726.5)
Cost of sales (indirect)	(1,150.5)	(1,354.9)	(1,420.2)	(1,480.1)	(1,540.0)	(1,579.5)
	7,803	7,958.6	8,133.3	8,713.4	9,093.5	9,694.0
Sales expenses	(1,950)	(1,950)	(1,870)	(1,790)	(1,710)	(1,630)
G&A	(2,980)	(2,980)	(2,980)	(2,980)	(2,980)	(2,980)
R&D	(810)	(846)	(838)	(837)	(837)	(837)
	2,063	2,182.6	2,445.3	3,106.4	3,566.5	4,247
Other income	(350)	(350)	(350)	(350)	(350)	(350)
Other expense	(235)	(235)	(235)	(235)	(235)	(235)
Interest expense	(225)	(191)	(150)	(100)	(50)	0
	1,953	2,106.6	2,410.3	3,121.4	3,631.5	4,362
Taxation	(781.2)	(842.6)	(964.1)	(1,248.5)	(1,452.6)	(1,744.8)
	1,171.8	1,264.0	1,446.2	1,872.9	2,178.9	2,617.2
Proposed dividend	0	(200)	(200)	(300)	(300)	(400)
	1,718.8	1,064.0	1,246.2	1,572.9	1,878.9	2,217.2
Prior retained earnings	19,153	20,324.8	21,388.8	22,635.0	24,207.9	26,086.8
Current retained earnings	20,324.8	21,388.8	22,635.0	24,207.9	26,086.8	28,304.0

TABLE 4.9 Flow of Funds Including Estimated Changes in Sales and Earnings Resulting from CAD/CAM Project
(in thousands of dollars)

	Year 1	Year 2	Year 3	Year 4	Year 5
Profit before taxation	2,106.6	2,410.3	3,121.4	3,631.5	4,362
Depreciation	1,920.4	1,941.2	1,761.6	1,382	1,382
Total funds	4,027	4,351.5	4,883	5,013.5	5,744
Dividend paid	0	(200)	(200)	(300)	(300)
Fixed asset investment	(102)	(104)	(102)	(102)	(0)
Taxation paid	(781.2)	(842.64)	(964.12)	(1,248.56)	(1,452.6)
Repayment of long-term debt	(680)	(820)	(1,000)	(1,000)	(1,000)
Increase in working capital	2,463.8	2,384.86	2,616.88	2,362.94	2,991.4
Movement in bank and cash	2,463.8	2,345.86	2,616.88	2,362.94	2,991.4

TABLE 4.10 Equity Value of the Company With and Without the CAD/CAM Project
(in thousands of dollars)

Year	Equity value without project	Equity value with project	Difference in equity value resulting from project
0	22,884	22,824	(60)
1	23,917	23,889	(28)
2	24,969	25,135	166
3	25,946	26,708	762
4	26,952	28,587	1635
5	27,889	30,804	2915

TABLE 4.11 Cash Generated for the Company With and Without the CAD/CAM Project
(in thousands of dollars)

Year*	Cash generated without project	Cash generated with project
1	2332	2464
2	2026	2385
3	1673	2617
4	1207	2364
5	1237	2991

*Net of investment cost, in thousands of dollars: year 0 = $700, year 1 = $302, year 2 = $341, year 3 = $377, year 4 = $417, year 5 = $354.

TABLE 4.12 Return on Investment of the CAD/CAM Project
(in thousands of dollars)

	Year 0	Year 1	Year 2	Year 3	Year 4	Year 5
Project cost	(700)	(302)	(340.5)	(377)	(416.5)	(354)
Benefit from project		360	680	1400	1920	2640
Tax benefit from project		40	(7.8)	(112.9)	(377.4)	(661.4)
Net cash flow	(700)	98	331.7	910.1	1126.1	1724.6
Return on investment = 62%						

```
         * WELCOME TO PEARS *
SELECT OPTION
* ENTER GENERAL INFORMATION
* ENTER COMPANY INFORMATION
* ENTER PROJECT INFORMATION
* PROCESS INFORMATION
* PRODUCE REPORTS
* HELP
* EXIT
```

Figure 4.1 The introductory screen for PEARS.

```
   * ENTER COMPANY INFORMATION *
SELECT OPTION
* ENTER   INFORMATION   LAYOUT
  TYPE
* DISPLAY INFORMATION LAYOUT
  TYPE
* ENTER  COMPANY  RESULTS  (IN
  ABSENCE OF PROJECT)
* MODIFY COMPANY RESULTS  (IN
  ABSENCE OF PROJECT)
* RETURN TO INTRODUCTORY MENU
* HELP
* EXIT
```

Figure 4.2 A second-level screen in PEARS.

Table 4.12 shows the calculation of the project's return on investment. To produce all these figures by hand is a long and painstaking process. Use of a program such as PEARS has many advantages. Figures 4.1 and 4.2 show examples of the easy-to-use interactive menus available with PEARS.

Chapter

5

People in the CAD/CAM Environment

As can be seen from Table 5.1, CAD/CAM affects many people throughout the company. It is an information-related technology (rather than a materials-related technology such as a machine tool), and people are the creators and users of information. This chapter looks at the effect of CAD/CAM on different people and the roles they must play. Those involved include top management (including the CAD/CAM director), financial management, middle and project management, the CAD/CAM manager and support staff, supervisors, direct users of CAD/CAM, indirect users of CAD/CAM, and nonusers of CAD/CAM. The role of the CAD/CAM champion is also discussed.

Without an understanding of the effect of CAD/CAM on people, or of the way in which they often respond to it, the CAD/CAM manager will not be able to offer much assistance. Since similar attitudes about CAD/CAM are held by people in many companies, knowledge of the behavior that has occurred in the past may help the CAD/CAM manager resolve some of the problems that will probably arise.

5.1 Top Management

Although the most obvious impact of CAD/CAM will be in the design engineering and manufacturing engineering departments, other departments such as production, purchasing, sales, and personnel will also be affected. It is therefore in the interests of the company that senior managers from all departments commit themselves to and understand the implementation of CAD/CAM. In part, this can be achieved through suitable training (as described in Chapter 10). However, it may also be necessary to modify some managers' goals to be sure that they actively promote effective use of CAD/CAM. As the or-

TABLE 5.1 People affected by CAD/CAM

Top management

Middle management
- Engineering
- Production
- EDP
- Finance
- Purchasing
- Marketing

CAD/CAM manager
- Support team

Direct users of CAD/CAM
- Engineers
- Drafters
- Supervisors

Indirect users
- Purchasing
- Marketing

ganization evolves to take advantage of CAD/CAM and as the relations between departments become more cooperative and less confrontational, some top managers may have to learn new skills and adopt new attitudes. Among the managers most likely to feel uncomfortable in the new climate, there are often those who believe that traditional methods are best and that computers and high technology create more problems than they solve. Unfortunately, the future is bleak for people who maintain such attitudes, since companies only have two choices—adapt to new circumstances or, like dinosaurs, go out of business.

Senior managers face a most challenging task because in addition to adapting themselves, they must also ensure that their staff adapt to new ways of working. Top management has an important role to play in leading other members of the company forward into the CAD/CAM era. In particular, senior managers will have to spend time with middle managers to explain the goals of the company and how CAD/CAM is intended to assist in meeting these goals, and to help them understand why they must change their own goals to meet the changing needs of the business. Top management must also be able to create the greatest possible cooperation between departments so that the benefits offered by CAD/CAM can be realized.

Top managers in this environment must recognize where the problems are likely to arise and be prepared to solve them in the interests of the company. The problems generated by the installation of high-technology equipment are almost always people-related and not technical. It is the management of people in a continuously changing environment, backed up by high technology, that is the challenge for top management today.

Within an organization there will be a number of people who, for a variety of reasons, do not want to change the way they work. Top management may use the introduction of CAD/CAM to force some of these changes to take place, as well as to provide the opportunity for others.

Experience shows that top management's commitment to CAD/CAM and its involvement in the CAD/CAM implementation, organization, and management processes are key factors leading to the successful use of CAD/CAM. If top management is unaware of the potential benefits of CAD/CAM and is not deeply involved in setting CAD/CAM objectives, it is quite possible that the final implementation will not correspond to the company's real requirements. Introduction of a suitable organizational structure is another activity that must be led by top management, since this is the only group of people with a global view of the company and the power to implement companywide changes.

Top management must continue to play a leading role in long-range planning for CAD/CAM. They will also be involved in long-range planning for computer integrated manufacturing (CIM); thus the implementation of CAD/CAM should occur within the context of CIM.

It may be difficult for top management, acting as a group, to carry out the role described above. It may be more suitable to appoint a CAD/CAM director—one person with total responsibility for the successful use of CAD/CAM. Whether this is a full-time role or a part-time role will depend on the size of the company and the degree of CAD/CAM penetration. The CAD/CAM director needs to be a high-level top manager whose authority is commensurate with the responsibilities of the task. The CAD/CAM director (responsible for CAD/CAM policy, procedures, and resources) should report directly to the chief executive officer or to a director with companywide responsibility for computers and information.

The CAD/CAM manager may find it difficult to convince top managers of the need for their involvement in CAD/CAM. The CAD/CAM manager has no authority over their behavior, and in the absence of a CAD/CAM director it may be impossible to obtain any practical support.

One approach that may be helpful is to arrange meetings between the company's top managers and top managers of companies successfully using CAD/CAM. Another is to publicize widely any examples of particularly effective use of CAD/CAM within the company. This may arouse the interest of a top manager wanting to be associated with successful developments in the company.

5.2 Financial Management

It may not be immediately obvious to the CAD/CAM manager why financial managers will be involved with CAD/CAM. The answer lies in investment appraisal and costing. In the past, many companies (and many engineers) have been dominated by financial analysts capable of producing a figure called *payback*. Payback, which was explained in Chapter 4, has often been considered as the key parameter in deciding the future of a project. Yet in the case of CAD/CAM, where the major benefits occur in the long term, payback is an inappropriate measure. In addition, it appears that in many companies the value of payback has been further reduced by the inability of financial analysts to do more than input into the payback formula the figures received from engineers and the inability of engineers to produce the figures that the analysts would like to receive. This is another example of the division of labor leading to overspecialization and a lack of understanding of real everyday issues. The result, in this case, is that the payback figure obtained appears to be meaningful because it was produced by the right administrative channels, yet may well have little meaning because neither the analyst nor the engineer has fully understood the real problem and its requirements.

Investment in CAD/CAM is investment in the long-term future of the company. The benefits that it will provide are not easy to estimate and associated costs are often hidden. It is unlikely that a financial manager with no understanding of a technology such as CAD/CAM will be able to make a sensible financial analysis of the CAD/CAM investment. Such managers will need to learn more about CAD/CAM and its relation to the future of the company so that they have a more balanced view. The CAD/CAM manager should ensure that financial managers are given suitable training.

Decisions will also have to be made about how the CAD/CAM investment will be recovered. Managers with no understanding of CAD/CAM are not likely to be able to make sensible decisions about how this should be done. In many cases they have loaded initial use of the system with high overhead and thus stifled its use.

Again, the CAD/CAM manager should make sure that suitable training is available, perhaps by inviting consultants to give presentations that include both the theoretical background and practical examples drawn from their experience with companies using CAD/CAM successfully. Sometimes, however, even after such training the financial analysts may still show little understanding. This may be because staff such as financial analysts are often very remote from the real activities of the business, are not closely associated with the success or failure of individual projects, and do not feel any need to understand new techniques. If this is the case, the CAD/CAM manager may need assistance from top management. Alternatively, the CAD/CAM manager may decide to learn enough about investment and cost analysis to be able to dispense with the financial analysts.

5.3 Middle Management

Resistance by middle managers, who may see CAD/CAM as a threat to their jobs, has often been a limiting factor in the successful implementation of CAD/CAM. Part of this resistance stems from a belief that since the computer appears to be taking over the product design function, it will not be long before it will also take over the associated management tasks. There is also a belief that if middle managers share information with other departments, then their power will be reduced. There is little basis for either belief. Certainly the role of the middle manager will change. It will change because the management of people using CAD/CAM is far more challenging than the management of people using drawing boards, because the CAD/CAM system is more powerful and complex than a drawing board. Thus there is the potential to do things much better but also for more things to go wrong. A manager who understands the business benefits that CAD/CAM can generate and can manage staff to achieve them will not have to worry about job security.

Middle managers have a key role to play in the successful implementation of CAD/CAM. They will often have to behave very differently than they have in the past, which will be much easier if they are fully aware of the reasons for introduction of CAD/CAM and have been involved in all stages of the implementation process.

Apart from the major role of managing people using or affected by the use of CAD/CAM, middle management will be involved in developing intermediate-term plans for CAD/CAM, in deciding which projects should make use of CAD/CAM, in making organizational changes to improve operating efficiency, and in making sure that the investment in CAD/CAM is recovered.

It takes time, however, for middle managers to adapt to the new environment. The CAD/CAM manager can help them in a variety of ways. The CAD/CAM manager can have direct discussions with middle management to try to understand and ease their worries. Suitable training should be available. The CAD/CAM manager should help top management in the process of redefining the goals of middle management so that due account is taken of the requirements of the CAD/CAM environment.

Middle managers must carry through the change from purely manual methods to a mixed CAD/CAM-manual environment and, ultimately, to a totally CAD/CAM environment. They must decide what is to be done with the CAD/CAM system and what is to be done manually. They must set targets and monitor the work being done on the system to ensure compliance with written procedures. They may be involved in the development and acceptance of new procedures.

Middle managers are also responsible for generating enthusiasm for CAD/CAM within their own department and for ensuring that everyone is working toward a common goal. This is important because there will be times when staff members are asked to perform tasks they do not like or agree with. For example, it may be that a certain assembly is to be designed on the CAD/CAM system. A designer may then be asked to develop a simple component of the assembly on the system. The designer may think it could be done quicker on the drawing board. It is up to the manager to gain support for the decision not to use the drawing board by explaining why the job should be done with CAD/CAM and what the benefits are to the company of doing it that way.

In performing their new role, middle managers require one fundamentally new skill—the understanding of CAD/CAM from both a business and a technical point of view. Substandard use of CAD/CAM has often resulted from the actions of managers who did not understand CAD/CAM, had no idea how to use CAD/CAM, and had no intention of learning how to operate the CAD/CAM system. It is vital to the success of a CAD/CAM implementation that middle managers learn at least the basics of operating the system and do not let it become a secret, closed world, known only to an elite group of individuals. The manager does not need to know how to design a complicated component but does need to know how to sign on to the system and access a model or a drawing. The manager also needs to know how to carry out other basic operations, such as interrogation of the database to find out the status of particular parts and drawings. (No drawing office manager would consider managing in an environment where it was not possible to look at the development of a design on the drawing board. In that respect there is no difference between CAD/CAM and manual techniques.)

The ability of the middle manager to use the CAD/CAM system will be seen as a sign of management commitment to CAD/CAM and will therefore have a beneficial effect on the majority of CAD/CAM users. It will also generate additional respect for the middle manager.

Some companies operate a project-oriented management structure in which the project manager has a key management role. In such an organization the role of the project manager is similar to that of the middle manager discussed above. The project manager must plan resource requirements, particularly the need for CAD/CAM workstations and experienced operators. In an organization where the demand for those resources is intense, such planning becomes a vital part of the project manager's function. In the implementation phase of CAD/CAM use, when managers and users are unfamiliar with new techniques and may have to work in a mixed CAD/CAM-manual environment, good project management is essential.

5.4 The CAD/CAM Manager

The CAD/CAM manager has a wide range of responsibilities and needs to have a wide range of talents. A background comprising experience in engineering and computer systems is most suitable. In addition, good organizing skills, good communications skills, and a mature and resilient personality are needed. The task is such, though, that even an exceptional person will need full support from top and middle management.

The CAD/CAM manager is responsible for the operations and development of the CAD/CAM system and for the procedures associated with its use. These procedures, described in more detail in Chapter 9, range from security of data to the keeping of system and user performance records.

The CAD/CAM manager is responsible for providing the company's engineers with the best CAD/CAM system, and the corresponding training and education, so that they can produce products that meet the company's goals. Although most of the individual, day-to-day tasks that are required to meet this objective will be carried out by members of the CAD/CAM team, the CAD/CAM manager will be held responsible for the everyday administration of CAD/CAM. This responsibility applies both to the good functioning and availability of the system and to the overall provision of CAD/CAM services in line with objectives set by top management. In the event that an effective CAD/CAM organization has not been set up, the results of CAD/CAM use will be substandard and will fail to meet objectives. The setting up of an organizational structure within which CAD/CAM can be used successfully is one of the first tasks of the CAD/CAM manager.

A user committee made up of representative users from different areas of the company should be set up. At regular intervals, the CAD/CAM manager should be formally invited to its meetings to discuss suggestions, complaints, and plans. It may also be useful for the

CAD/CAM manager to formally arrange meetings of a middle-management committee during which intermediate-term plans concerning projects, training, system development, interface development, and introduction of CAD/CAM to new areas can be discussed. The fact that these committees exist does not imply that there should be no other communication between the CAD/CAM manager, the users, and middle management. On the contrary, direct, informal dialogue is essential.

The CAD/CAM manager must report periodically to top management on the actual use of CAD/CAM relative to original objectives. Intermediate-term plans and budgets should be presented and assistance given for the company's long-term plans.

The CAD/CAM manager should be selected as early as possible so that he or she will be aware of the reasons behind choices that are made, be able to participate in making these choices, and be able to increase the commitment to these choices. Choices made early on, such as priority of projects, system selection, ergonomics, and training, all need long-term support.

In some ways, the CAD/CAM manager acts as a bridge between the engineering departments and the EDP department. Before the advent of CAD/CAM systems, most engineering computing was carried out on the company's mainframe computers under the control of the EDP department. Engineers sometimes wrote small FORTRAN programs to run on the mainframe, but the bulk of the software was written by programmers in the EDP department. The introduction of CAD/CAM has led to changes. Since computer graphics and geometric modeling require considerable amounts of processing power, most CAD/CAM is not carried out on the company's mainframe computer, but on a separate mainframe computer or workstation. This computer will usually be physically situated in an engineering department, out of the jurisdiction of the EDP department. Generally it will be managed and run by members of the engineering department with little reference to the EDP department. Many EDP managers have felt their control and influence being severely threatened by such developments and have tried to assert their responsibility for CAD/CAM. In general, though, they have not succeeded, and the policy of placing the responsibility for the CAD/CAM system with the management of engineering users (and, in particular, with the CAD/CAM manager) has continued.

The CAD/CAM manager can therefore be seen as a supplier of computer services. It is somewhat paradoxical that a person who is probably a skilled engineer is not responsible for engineering, but for the provision of computer services, and reports not to EDP management but to engineering management. This problem has been mentioned in earlier chapters. It will disappear in time as the use of CAD/CAM in engineering becomes as important and widespread as that of EDP in the financial and administrative departments. It would then appear equally anomalous for the CAD/CAM manager to report to EDP.

The CAD/CAM manager will be supported by the CAD/CAM team, the size of which will depend on the size of the installation. The team members are usually drawn from the engineering departments where they were once the leading CAD/CAM users. (The progression from lead user to CAD/CAM team to CAD/CAM manager is a fairly typical career path in many companies.) The responsibilities of the CAD/CAM team include training, overseeing system backup, managing plotters, evaluating new hardware and software, managing system development, assisting users with particular problems, providing day-to-day vendor liaison, developing procedures, and acting as a first line of defense when faults occur on the system. The CAD/CAM manager must lead and motivate the CAD/CAM team members.

5.5 The Supervisor

In essence, the introduction of CAD/CAM does not change the role of the supervisor, although the supervisor's perception of the role may change. Care must be taken to avoid the situation that has arisen in many companies where the supervisor has stood back from the system, failed to get involved, and left staff to get on with it as best they could. For many companies this behavior has been disastrous, often resulting in expensive terminals sitting idle gathering dust in the corner.

In a CAD/CAM environment, just as in the world of the drawing board, the manager must manage and the supervisor must supervise. This implies that supervisors must understand CAD/CAM and know how to operate the system. Every supervisor directly responsible for managing users of a CAD/CAM system should complete a basic training course and be capable of designing to a limited degree. This is the only way that the supervisor will be able to understand what staff members are doing, and the only way he or she will be able to understand their problems and help solve them.

Once the system is in place, the CAD/CAM manager should provide suitable training for supervisors and make sure that they take advantage of it as soon as possible. Otherwise supervisors will be soon outdistanced by system users.

5.6 Direct Users of CAD/CAM

There is no single definition of a direct user of CAD/CAM. In its broadest sense, the term is used to describe those who use computers to help carry out engineering work leading to the creation of engineering information. They do not necessarily make use of graphics screens. People such as designers, drafters, supervisors, checkers, part programmers, and process planners are included in the category of direct users of CAD/CAM.

Direct users tend to fall into two fairly clear-cut categories: those who are very enthusiastic about CAD/CAM and those who are very much opposed to it. In the initial stages of CAD/CAM use (when it is very important to succeed), the CAD/CAM manager will need to rely on people in the first group. However, in the long run, it may be necessary to train some of the others as well. Many large companies who have taken the policy decision to train all potential users have found that, given enough time and good training, almost all trainees—regardless of age, sex, race, and creed—can learn to use CAD/CAM.

The first group see that the introduction of CAD/CAM presents a series of new opportunities in terms of making the job more enjoyable and offering new career prospects. They feel that work can become more enjoyable because so many more alternatives are possible and because much of the routine work will be done by the system. Such people are prepared to learn new skills, carry out a wider range of jobs, and accept flexible working hours. They are often deeply committed to their work and will try to make the best possible use of CAD/CAM regardless of the shortcomings of the system and the way that it has been implemented. Generally, these users accept that the introduction of CAD/CAM will lead to a requirement for a more formalized and structured approach to the organization of work.

Furthermore, they will support the introduction of procedures that must be strictly adhered to in order that the overall benefits resulting from the introduction of CAD/CAM can be easily achieved. The major difficulties that the CAD/CAM manager will have with such people are restraining them from doing too much too soon and making sure that they receive sufficient support in the areas of training, documentation, and interfaces.

The second group of users are often not supportive of the new ways of working because of fear resulting from a lack of understanding and involvement. Typically, they will find it difficult to keep up with the training course. They will complain about the physical characteristics of the graphics screen and about any functions of the system that do not exactly correspond to their previous experience. They will find it very difficult to get used to a more formalized and structured approach to the organization of work, particularly if, in the past, standard procedures did not exist or were not rigorously enforced.

The most effective way for the CAD/CAM manager to make sure

that the number of people in the second group is as low as possible is by taking positive actions well before the system is installed. As early as possible in the CAD/CAM implementation decision process, users and nonusers should be involved. They should be given awareness training to ensure that they understand CAD/CAM and appreciate why the company is implementing such a technology. They need to understand that, for their own good, they need to be adaptable, that the company is in business to make money, and that the CAD/CAM system is just one of many tools supporting that objective. They need to be made aware of the possibilities that there will be for them to develop their abilities and improve their career prospects. Once the system is installed and in use, the CAD/CAM manager and middle managers should identify people who have negative attitudes toward CAD/CAM and try to help them to have a more positive view. In the end, though, it may be that these people realize themselves, by looking around and seeing the results their colleagues obtain, that it is time they too took advantage of the opportunities of the situation.

5.7 Indirect Users of CAD/CAM

Indirect users of CAD/CAM are those that do not directly create engineering information but use engineering information created by others in their own work. Examples are people in marketing and purchasing. In the CAD/CAM environment, the indirect users are as important as the users. The indirect users will either be part of a department working alongside CAD/CAM users, or they will be in a department which interfaces with user departments. In either case, they need to know what role the system is performing and how it will affect their functioning. Sometimes, for example, the indirect user may be required to sit next to a user and discuss some aspect of the design displayed on the workstation. The indirect user may also benefit from immediate access to data from a terminal, where once it was necessary to wait for information to arrive in the internal mail.

The CAD/CAM manager should make sure the activities of indirect users are considered during the definition of the company's CAD/CAM requirements. Indirect users should be made aware of the pending introduction of CAD/CAM and the reasons for it. Once the system has been installed, the CAD/CAM manager should make sure that they receive suitable training and are kept informed of new developments. As the introduction of CAD/CAM may lead to significant modifications in the job content of some indirect users, the CAD/CAM manager and the managers of indirect users should work together to identify and implement improvements.

5.8 CAD/CAM Nonusers

There will be many people in the company who will be neither directly nor indirectly affected by the introduction and use of CAD/CAM. It does not follow that they should be ignored by the CAD/CAM manager and completely excluded from all information concerning CAD/CAM. This is partly because the CAD/CAM manager needs to develop support for CAD/CAM throughout the company and partly because, as the use of CAD/CAM increases, many people who were previously seen as nonusers will become either direct or indirect users. They will have a more positive attitude to the use of CAD/CAM if they have been kept aware of its previous progress. The CAD/CAM manager should therefore give brief CAD/CAM awareness presentations to nonusers.

5.9 The CAD/CAM Champion

Every company needs to have a CAD/CAM champion. The champion will be a passionate believer in the benefits of CAD/CAM and will do all possible to make sure that it is introduced and used successfully. Such a person needs to have a good understanding not only of the company itself, but of the benefits that CAD/CAM can bring to the company and the way to achieve those benefits. The champion will be resolute in believing in CAD/CAM and determined to make it work, even though both management and users may put up strong resistance.

The CAD/CAM champion has to be able to sell the idea of CAD/CAM to top management, make it work in practice, and ensure that benefits are achieved. In principle, the champion can be at any level of the company, but clearly it will be more beneficial to the company if a director rather than a junior manager champions the cause. Of course, if there is more than one champion, then, provided that they work together, the end result should be even more impressive. The ideal solution would be that the CAD/CAM director, the CAD/CAM manager, and some individual users all champion the CAD/CAM cause in their own areas. If, on the other hand, the only champion is the CAD/CAM manager, it would be essential to try to identify and strengthen supporters of CAD/CAM among top management and users.

Chapter

6

Selection and Sizing of CAD/CAM Hardware and Software

This chapter looks at the activities that should take place between the moment that a company first decides to invest in CAD/CAM and the moment that top management decides on a specific solution. The activities are grouped into 14 steps, which are shown in Table 6.1.

6.1 Feasibility Study

Many companies take 1, 2, or even 3 years to select a CAD/CAM solution. Another 3 or 4 years may then go by before it becomes clear that the investment has paid off. Unless top management understands from the very beginning of the CAD/CAM implementation process that this is a long-term activity with a long-term payback, it may be

TABLE 6.1 Fourteen Steps to Selecting a CAD/CAM Solution

1	Feasibility study
2	Setting up a task force
3	Information buildup
4	Description of the current situation
5	Definition of requirements
6	Understanding available hardware and software
7	Writing the request for proposal
8	Definition of selection criteria
9	Preparation of the first short list. Sending the RFP
10	Receipt of replies. The final short list
11	Detailed evaluation of the hot solutions
12	Simulation of the hot solutions
13	Analysis of evaluation and simulation
14	Decision

decided—out of frustration—to terminate the process before the hoped-for results are achieved. A feasibility study carried out right at the beginning of the process can reduce this danger by making clear to management that not only will there be no payback for a long time, but that the process of choosing a solution is also lengthy and costly.

The feasibility study should be done quickly, saving both time and money. To gain management respect, someone who is both neutral and expert should carry it out. Often, this means that the feasibility study will have to be carried out by someone from outside the company.

6.2 Setting Up a Task Force

CAD/CAM is a companywide activity. The investigation into its use should be carried out by a task force made up of about six people coming from different parts of the company. The exact composition of the task force will depend on the staff available and the areas where CAD/CAM may be used. Typically, though, it would include a design engineer, a drafter, a manufacturing engineer, and one person from the finance, EDP, production, and marketing departments. It would be beneficial if the future CAD/CAM manager were a member of the task force, but this person may not yet have been identified. The task force leader should be a forward-looking, respected manager. Depending on the size of the company, participation in task force activities may be a part-time or full-time job. When the task force is set up, it should be given clear directives as to its goals, its schedule, and its authority. Given this information, the task force should be able to establish a detailed plan of activities and a corresponding timetable. A typical example is shown in Table 6.2. Note that time for decision making has to be included in the plan.

6.3 Information Buildup

One of the first activities of the task force is to increase the level of CAD/CAM knowledge in the company so that a reasoned selection of solutions can be made. It may be a good idea for all members of the task force to attend an introductory course on CAD/CAM so that they all start off with at least some basic knowledge and so that they can all talk the same language. Information can also be gathered from reading journals, magazines, and books; by attending conferences, exhibitions, and vendor demonstrations; and by visiting users of CAD/CAM.

Other members of the company who will be affected by the implementation should be informed that a modernization of work methods

TABLE 6.2 Timetable for Task Force Activities

Date	Action
	Year 0
September 30	Introductory course completed.
December 16	Draft preliminary report presented to management. Contents include: current situation, requirements, outline solutions, revised plan, and timetable for year 1.
	Year 1
January 13	Taking account of management reaction, definitive version of preliminary report produced.
March 24	Draft of detailed requirements document and proposed vendor short list presented to top management.
May 5	Taking account of management reaction, definitive version of detailed requirements document produced. Definitive vendor short list drawn up.
May 26	Request for proposal document produced and sent to short-listed vendors.
June 16	System evaluation procedures defined.
June 30	Last day for vendor replies.
July 14	RFP replies and final short list of three vendors reported to management.
July 28	Technical benchmarks set up.
September 15	Technical benchmarks terminated .
October 6	Other evaluation procedures completed.
October 27	Final report presented to management.

is under review. They should be kept informed of progress. Similarly management should also be kept up-to-date. The more that management understands about CAD/CAM, the more it will be able to contribute positively toward future activities.

Information buildup is a continuous activity. Clearly the task force needs to be sufficiently well informed before proposing a solution, but the process does not stop there. More information—some of it more detailed, some of it relating to other subjects—will be needed for the following activities. As well as learning more about CAD/CAM, the task force will need to learn more about the way the company works and progress to a point at which it is possible to define the company's CAD/CAM requirements.

6.4 Description of the Current Situation

The description of the current situation and the definition of requirements, although presented sequentially here, are complementary activities and can be carried out in parallel by the task force. The description of the current situation covers six areas: the company's engineering and manufacturing information flow, application areas, organization, people, work modes, and computers.

CAD/CAM is a technique that should lead to an improvement in the quality, use, and communication of engineering information. The task force must understand how the engineering and manufacturing activities of the company make use of information. This should not be done through a top-down functional decomposition, but by following the various product paths and identifying for each activity the input, use, creation, storage, and output of information. A typical new product path might start in marketing and then continue through conceptual design, engineering design and analysis, testing, detailed design, production planning, process planning, tooling, NC programming, machining, assembly, quality control, testing, packaging, distribution, and after-sales. There will be other product paths for modified designs originating from marketing, design engineering, and manufacturing engineering staff. Activities that occur outside the company, carried out perhaps by partners or suppliers, should also be considered. The task force will gain a good understanding of the overall flow and use of information from this exercise.

At the same time, the task force should address the individual activities, such as engineering design, process planning, and NC programming. These are potential CAD/CAM application areas. The current activity in each application area should be understood in terms of both individual tasks and numbers describing use of engineering information (such as number of new products, number of modified products, number of drawings modified, number of times a part is modified, and so on).

Some information should also be gathered on the complexity of the work: Is it a matter of simple parts or complicated machines? Are only detail drawings produced, or are there assembly drawings as well? How many of each? Are there parts lists on both types of drawings, or just on one? Are the products mass produced, are they one-of-a-kind, are there families of products? Similarly, information should be gathered concerning the standards adhered to within each activity and the control procedures that are in place for tasks such as drawing management.

The current organization of the company needs to be described from the CAD/CAM point of view. The description will show where the potential users are, in terms of both organization and geography. It should also look at the need for information transfer from the same point of view and comment upon any factors that may hinder flow.

The people who will be the future users of CAD/CAM should be identified. An attempt should be made to describe their current skills and their willingness and ability to use CAD/CAM. The working modes of these people should be understood, as these can greatly affect the choice of system. There may be a group of people primarily involved in conceptual design and advanced development work. Another group may be involved in engineering design and the accompanying analysis tasks such as structural analysis or simulation. There may be a group that is mainly involved in modification. Their work may involve making slight adaptations to existing products. The groups mentioned above could be focused on mechanical design or electronic design, or could be multidisciplinary.

The final part of the description of the current situation involves the company's use of computers. There are two reasons for this. One is that in a company that has already successfully introduced computers, CAD/CAM may avoid some of the basic obstacles that the first computer in a company always seems to find. The other is related to the exchange of information between CAD/CAM and other areas of the company. Because a primary objective of introducing CAD/CAM is to improve the information flow, it is necessary to investigate the current state of some of the other computer-based information sources that may provide, or make use of, CAD/CAM data. Among these are production planning systems (such as MRP), factory control systems, part programming systems (for NC, CNC, DNC), analysis programs (such as finite element analysis), quality control systems, and last but not least, the company's finance and administration computer.

6.5 Definition of Requirements

The aim of this activity is to understand the basic requirements of management and potential CAD/CAM users and to translate this understanding into a formal report. This report serves to increase the overall understanding of CAD/CAM and to identify areas of disagreement that must be resolved. It should assign priorities to the requirements and define which are essential. In its agreed form it will serve as a major input for the request for proposal. A company that has never prepared such a report may benefit from the assistance of an expert in the field.

Without management involvement this activity will be almost worthless. CAD/CAM is a technique that will affect the long-term future of the company. The solution chosen should be in harmony with the company's strategic objectives. Will the company stay in the same industrial sector? Will it diversify? Will it retain the same product range? Will metals in products be replaced by plastics? Will there be a major electronics component in future products? These questions are necessary since current CAD/CAM systems are generally either limited in capability or industry-specific. As a result, a system that would be ideal for a company heavily involved in composites might be of little value to a plastic molder. Similarly, if the company intends to close down the engineering department or withdraw a major product line, the requirements for CAD/CAM will change.

It is important to understand management's view of the strategic importance of CAD/CAM. Is it only to be used to produce drawings faster? Is it seen as a major part of an overall strategy aimed at the introduction of integrated manufacturing techniques? What benefits does management hope to achieve from using CAD/CAM—reduced costs, improved design, or what? What are the priorities associated with these expected benefits? What level of ROI is management looking for?

To obtain the above information, the task force will question managers who should have the answers. However, to obtain the answers to questions pertaining to future use of CAD/CAM, the task force may have some problems since the users may have little feeling for future CAD/CAM requirements. At this stage, the task force may call for assistance from an outside expert, or may try to answer the questions on the basis of its collective knowledge.

There will be questions to answer concerning the application areas to which CAD/CAM should be applied and the order in which it is applied to them. Similarly, the task force will have to know what percentage of work in each area will be carried out by CAD/CAM initially and over what period will this percentage rise, eventually eliminating manual work altogether. What figures are realistic? In mechanical engineering in 1988 there are few users who spend 100 percent of their time in front of a screen. The percentage is more likely to be between 25 and 75 percent, although there are many who register an even lower figure. No doubt, in time, these figures will increase, as they have done for electronic engineering where CAE systems are much more advanced. At some time, expert systems will start to play an important role in engineering, but their effect is currently very difficult to estimate.

There are also various integration requirements to be considered. On one hand, the interfaces with production planning, NC machines, and other computer-based systems have to be defined. On the other hand, the relationships with suppliers, partners, and important clients have to be considered. Management and user requirements must be "integrated." A management requirement to develop families of products should match with a corresponding user requirement for parametric design.

The final report on the requirements is an important document defining in clearly understandable terms why CAD/CAM is being introduced, the way in which it will be used, and the impact that it will have. Basic principles should be explained, any major assumptions discussed, and potential problem areas highlighted.

The report should contain a prioritized list of the system functions required. The associated flow and use of information should be described. The report should describe interfaces with other systems that will be required. It should also include a statement of the scope and content of work to be carried out by CAD/CAM and associated timings and volumes. This information will be of importance when defining the size of the installation.

Production of such a report will show that the task force has met one of its major goals. The report itself will help to promote better understanding of CAD/CAM throughout the company.

6.6 Available Hardware and Software

By this time, the task force should have developed a reasonable knowledge of available CAD/CAM hardware and software. (If not, it should take some crash courses, visit exhibitions, and ask vendors to demonstrate their wares.) As there are at least a thousand combinations of available hardware and software packages, this is not the place to describe them. Instead, some comments will be made about trends in CAD/CAM hardware and software.

Computers are becoming smaller, cheaper, and more powerful, thus allowing the use of more complex engineering systems based on artificial intelligence techniques. Graphics terminals and workstations will become cheaper yet have more local intelligence. There will be a tendency for each user to want a personal workstation, which will probably have a fairly low resolution graphics screen and be connected to a local area network. The network will also contain computer servers, disk servers, and so on. "Office automation" functions will be available on the same workstation. The engineering environment will become much more "computerized." There will be less emphasis on the "CAs" (representing computer-aided) in CAD/CAM, since, as a matter of course, all tasks will be computer aided.

In the same way, the debate about PC-based CAD/CAM, which occurred in the late 1980s, will die away. Once the market has shaken down, PCs will be seen to be, like engineering workstations, desktop tools for engineering professionals. They will not radically change the basics of CAD/CAM, such as geometric modeling and reuse of information. They will not do away with the need for an organization that fits the new technological environment, nor will they eliminate the need for training, procedures, and properly constructed engineering databases.

Other peripherals will also undergo rapid development. Optical disks with 70 Gbytes memory will be available. Memory will be cheap enough to be decentralized, thus creating a need for very complex data management systems. Scanners will be available to automatically input manually produced or CAD/CAM-produced drawings. The use of networks will spread as users and vendors combine to translate standards such as manufacturing automation protocol (MAP), technical office protocol (TOP), and open systems interconnect (OSI) into effective use. Solid modelers will be used more widely once they become easier to use, handle sculptured surfaces, provide better response times, and perform better for simple tasks such as drafting.

CAD/CAM systems will become more open, and it will be possible for them to communicate with other CAD/CAM systems, non-engineering systems, and all sorts of central and distributed databases. Facilities will be available for users to easily and comfortably add their own functions.

Increased standardization incorporated in software will overcome the current need to develop a special interface for almost every pair of systems. Data transfer between systems and between a system and a peripheral will become transparent. Powerful engineering data management systems will become available. Users will have rapid access through a single terminal to all the data they require. Data input devices will be improved to facilitate data input. The mouse, the menu, the tablet, and voice recognition will replace most other devices currently in use.

The use of expert systems will radically change the task of the engineer, but it is currently difficult to forecast when such systems will be widely available commercially, and even more difficult to forecast when the typical engineer will be able to use them. (It is interesting to note that 25 years after the first use of CAD/CAM, only a minority of engineers use the technique.)

Finally, it can be expected that the price of most CAD/CAM software will continue to fall. When all PC-based drafting systems have the same functionality, price becomes the major competitive weapon of their suppliers. Only the high-end systems offering functions not available elsewhere will be able to maintain price levels.

6.7 Writing the Request for Proposal

The basis for the request for proposal (RFP) is the report containing the company's CAD/CAM requirements. It is probably the only formal document describing the company's requirements that a vendor will receive. As such, it is in the company's interest that it be as complete as possible so that the vendor can gain a clear understanding of what is required. Typically it will contain a description of the company, its business and its products, a description of what the system is to be used for, an estimate of the size of the installation, the objectives of system use, and the critical factors describing the required system (such as number of parts, geographic constraints, and number of users).

As a request for proposal can run to more than 100 pages, details of the contents will not be given here. Among the major items to be considered are hardware, software, data management, data communications, user-friendliness, training, integration, documentation, assistance, development, maintenance, application areas to be addressed, functions required in each application area, installation constraints, and implementation timetable.

6.8 Definition of Selection Criteria

Before sending out the request for proposal (an action usually followed by an instant siege by the vendor's top sales people), the task force should define (without vendor influence) the criteria for choosing a particular solution. The major input for this activity will be the requirements report.

There are four types of criteria to be considered—technical, economic, vendor, and organizational. Generally, about 15 major technical criteria can be identified, as well as between 5 and 10 major criteria for each of the three other types. A "relative importance factor" should be assigned to each of the criteria; for example, if only three criteria are considered, documentation may be given a factor of 25, training 200, and functionality of the initial system 1000; thus functionality is seen to be 40 times as important as documentation. Systems will be evaluated against these factors. A system that offers 20 percent of requirements in documentation, 15 percent in training, and 80 percent in functionality will score 5 + 30 + 800; i.e., 835, whereas a system offering 100 percent of requirements in documentation, 100 percent in training, and 75 percent in functionality will score 25 + 200 + 750, i.e., 975. The latter system, scoring higher by a large margin, would be selected.

This method of selection allows the task force to take account of a large range of criteria of differing importance. The choice of criteria and the "relative importance factors" are clearly crucial to the selection process and should be made solely on the basis of the company's requirements as expressed in the requirements report.

6.9 Preparation of the First Short List: Sending the RFP

By now the task force will have clearly identified the CAD/CAM requirements of the company. During its peregrinations it will have come into contact with very many systems. (A visit to a major exhibition provides the chance to see at least 20 systems, and a CAD/CAM magazine will probably refer to more than 50.) The task force should use its knowledge of the market and of company requirements to make a short list of the six or seven most likely vendors. The RFP should be sent to them.

6.10 Receipt of Replies: The Final Short List

The vendors should have replied within a month. Many of them will have been in telephone contact and tried to arrange visits. Whether the proposals for visits are accepted depends on the task force. In theory, all vendors should be treated equally at this stage, and the intention is not to arrange visits with all the vendors. On the other hand, there may be, in practice, good reasons for such visits.

The task force should judge the vendor replies strictly against the selection criteria. A final short list of the three most suitable potential solutions should be drawn up for more detailed evaluation.

6.11 Detailed Evaluation of the Hot Solutions

Any one of the three "hot" solutions would probably be suitable. The detailed evaluation is carried out to increase familiarity with these systems to the point that they have been fully understood and that there is no doubt about their proving successful in operational use.

The four types of criteria considered before—technical, economic, vendor, and organizational—will be retained. Neither the criteria nor the relative importance factors need to be modified, as they represent the company's requirements. The scores of an individual system for particular criteria may change as understanding of that system increases.

A deeper understanding of the systems is best gained through practical use, by a procedure that is commonly known as a benchmark test. The proposed benchmark test should be identical for each system. It should be directly related to the type of work that the company would carry out on the system. It should be well prepared by the task force so that only about 1 day would be required to test each system. The task force should aim to develop a simple but revealing test of the systems that clarifies their understanding of the system's capabilities in areas that are crucial to the company. These areas will differ from one company to another but will probably cover more than one application and could, for example, include three-dimensional modeling, two-dimensional design, parametrics, parts list generation, NC program generation, and engineering data management.

The result of a benchmark test should be treated with caution. It must be remembered that the test is carried out to learn more about a system, not to find fault with it. Poor benchmark performance may be due to all sorts of things; e.g., the person the vendor assigns to the benchmark may lack a particular skill or there may be an unnoticed error in test preparation. Once the benchmarks have been completed it will probably be useful to check, and modify if necessary, the scores assigned to the key criteria.

Among the most important technical criteria reviewed may be geometric modeling, data management, user interface, potential interfaces to other systems and computers, functions in particular application areas, and customization possibilities. It may not be possible to cover all aspects in a 1-day benchmark test. Therefore, rather than spending more time on benchmark tests, it may be more suitable to seek the advice of a neutral expert who has experience with the real-life characteristics of several systems.

The most important economic criteria could include: costs for the total system, maintenance, new versions, installation, and additional workstations; expected increase in sales; expected decreases in product costs; and ROI.

The most important vendor criteria could include commitment to CAD/CAM, development plans, ability to upgrade hardware and software, maintenance record, delivery time, availability of technical assistance, growth record, and user group. Organizational criteria to be considered include system installation, system management, training, system support, implementation of standards, development of libraries, data access, data security, archiving, data lookup, and quality control.

6.12 Simulation of the Hot Solutions

Rather than limiting themselves to working out the ratings of the hot solutions, the task force should also investigate the way in which each of these would be implemented and used over the first year. Major subjects of investigation should include the organization of people and data, the determination of system size, and development of a 1-year plan for installation and use.

As the CAD/CAM organization and the roles of people have been mentioned in previous chapters, they do not need to be described in detail here. It is clear, though, that these are both very important subjects. The roles, skill requirements, training, and reporting channels of drafters, engineers, part programmers, and support staff need to be identified.

Similarly, the organization of data is discussed in detail in another chapter. Again, though, it is an important subject, and the task force would do well to try to anticipate the result of the first year's use; transmission, exchange, modification, storage, archiving, and recall of data; and the corresponding requirements for security, access, and integrity.

The size of the initial system configuration is always a problem. On the one hand, there is a tendency to reduce the risk; on the other hand, there is the need to make a noticeable impact. The configuration will also depend on the size of the company, the number of potential users, and the tasks they will carry out on the system. One CAE workstation for the only electronics engineer in a small company may produce electrifying results. However, in a much larger company with hundreds of engineers, it would have little effect on the overall flow of engineering information.

To get some feeling for the figures, it can be estimated that one workstation will probably handle the work of two or three average users (i.e., those who spend less than 50 percent of their time at the screen). A company with 10 potential users might decide to start with two workstations on the assumption that system use will result in a "productivity gain" of two, resulting in some of the users being laid off. However, productivity gain calculations of this type are very suspect, particularly because in practice companies that invest in CAD/CAM rarely lay off skilled engineering staff. Looking at initial system size from a different point of view, it is noteworthy that companies that are now users of CAD/CAM have often started with one workstation for more than 20 potential users.

The task force should make sure that the initial configuration can be expanded without too much disruption. Many companies have found that their installations double in size every few years. There is no point in buying a small cheap configuration that will have to be scrapped and replaced after 2 or 3 years. This process is expensive from many points of view. It will probably result in loss of much of the data entered on the system and lead to retraining of users.

As a final part of the simulation, the task force should define a 1-year plan for installation and use of each of the hot solutions. Each plan should show who will be trained and when, which applications will be developed first and when, which projects will benefit or suffer from use of CAD/CAM, and so on.

6.13 Analysis of Evaluation and Simulation

Having carried out thorough evaluations and simulations of the hot solutions, the task force should be in a position to decide which is their preferred solution. They should prepare a report for management recalling the objectives of CAD/CAM, the criteria developed, the results of tests carried out, and the reasons for their choice. In particular, the benefits and costs of the proposed solution should be spelled out, as should the proposed implementation plan. The reasons for rejecting the other solutions should also be described.

6.14 Decision

It is management that must take the final decision. Management will often try to reduce the risk by cutting down the scale of the task force's proposal. In some cases, this may be justified, but task forces are generally cautious organizational entities and watering down their proposal may result in a very ineffective implementation of CAD/CAM.

If management feels very unhappy about the advisability of investing in CAD/CAM, there should be no hesitation in saying so. It may well be that this is not the best time to invest in CAD/CAM. There is no point in going ahead with a project that is destined to fail just because it appears to follow the latest technological trend.

Chapter 7

CAD/CAM in the Company—Year 1

The year that follows the introduction of CAD/CAM is often very difficult and full of mixed emotions. In many cases, people throughout the company will start the year with a particular view of CAD/CAM and end it with a different one. Top management will want to see a rapid return on investment, but, as this is unlikely, by the end of the year they will be disillusioned and no longer supportive. Middle management will start the year looking for short-term productivity gains, but, as these rarely occur, they will probably finish the year treating CAD/CAM as the root of all evil. The engineering staff will start the year somewhat fearful of the introduction of a new technique, but will end it wondering what all the fuss was about. Labor unions will start the year worrying about the effect that CAD/CAM may have on their members, but by the end of the year will probably regret that management did not introduce it earlier. The only way to try to overcome these changes of attitude, and the problems that they lead to, is to make sure that even before the system is chosen people really understand what CAD/CAM can and cannot do.

7.1 The Purchase Order

Following top management's decision to invest in CAD/CAM, the next step will be to prepare the purchase order, procurement contract, and accompanying documents. This will be the responsibility of the CAD/CAM manager, who should have been appointed by now. The CAD/CAM manager is not expected to carry out all the tasks associated with the purchase order since many of them are clearly the responsibility of the finance and administration staff. However, the CAD/CAM manager is responsible for the detailed technical aspects and for making sure that the overall requirements of management are respected. The purchase order must also be acceptable to vendor management. When the two sets of management are in agreement, the contract will be signed.

It will probably take some time to get to this stage. One of the major reasons for the holdup is that the company realizes again that it is about to enter into purchase of a system from a perhaps unknown vendor with whom close relations will be necessary over at least the next 5 years. The company will want to double check that it is making the right decision, and in doing so may decide to modify its requirements slightly. The company is purchasing the system for the long term, so it is not unreasonable to spend a few weeks making sure that the right system is being purchased, that it really will do what it is expected to do, that it is bought as cheaply as is reasonably possible, and that the foundations of a good long-term relationship with the vendor are being put in place.

Development of the detailed documentation accompanying the purchase order will make it clear to the company what it really wants and will also show the vendor what is really required. It is better that misunderstandings appear and are resolved at this stage, rather than after system installation. From the point of view of purchase, the company should make it clear just what it wants to buy in the way of CPUs; peripherals, such as screens; and software. Some of these items may be regarded by the vendor as part of a standard package; some may be thought of as extras. The company must specify in detail at which sites the system will be used since different vendors have different attitudes to multisite installations. Similarly, the company should make clear its intentions to purchase interfaces, training, and documentation. Again, some of these items may be included in the standard price; others may not. The expected delivery date, acceptance procedures, and any associated penalties should also be included. Conversions (for example, of NC postprocessors) should be clearly defined, along with the corresponding responsibilities for development and testing and corresponding ownership rights. The amount of support that the vendor will supply under the standard terms of purchase should be stated. The amount and cost of additional support should be described separately. During the long process of selection, there may have been mention of volume discounts, trade allowances, discounts for being part of a major corporation, discounts for agreeing to carry out joint developments, and so on. Now is the time to put these on paper.

The maintenance and service part of the contract should be looked at in detail. There is a wide range of options. At one end are time-and-materials contracts in which the vendor is only paid for service provided when requested. At the other end are 24-hour full-service contracts for which the vendor will make a flat-rate monthly charge that is independent of the amount of service given. The annual cost of such service may well be over 10 percent of the total purchase price. In between the two extremes are all sorts of possibilities that allow the company to pay the price that it wants or to have the service that it wants; unfortunately, the two rarely coincide. It may be possible for the company to do some of its own maintenance, particularly preventive maintenance. If this is to be the case, it should be mentioned in the contract. Other subjects to be covered include the maximum repair time for major parts and a contingency plan (perhaps the supply of a replacement system) should this time be exceeded. Details should be given of the services that are included in the maintenance contract, as well as the cost of those that are excluded.

There will be some eventualities that will not be covered by the maintenance contract, and they may need to be covered by a separate insurance contract. Some of the eventualities may be covered under existing insurance of computer equipment, but it is wise to check the situation with regard to hardware theft and damage, fire, power outages, software corruption of data, and so on.

To make sure that unintentional loopholes do not remain in the contract, a lawyer who understands the legal aspects of computer and software contracts should be asked to check it over. Similarly, the finance and administration people will want to look in detail at the purchase and maintenance conditions to see if it would not be to the company's cash flow and/or tax advantage to rent, lease, or otherwise obtain the system.

So far, it has been assumed that there is only one vendor. If there is more than one, then the situation will probably be more complicated. It may be possible to get one of the vendors to take a leading role, with the others being subcontractors. Alternatively, it may be necessary to deal with several vendors separately. In this case it is important to make sure that each one is made responsible for providing hardware and software that works with the rest of the system. Again, this must be clearly defined in the contract. The intention is not to avoid paying the vendors, but to put in place the rules by which they will be paid provided that they do what they have promised to do. In all cases it is preferable to make a series of payments, rather than a single lump-sum payment. The first payment will probably be made at the time of contract signature and another at installation time. The final payment should be made after the system has been working as promised for 2 months. Again, this is not meant to penalize the vendor, but to act as a reminder that a long-term commitment has been entered into and must be taken seriously by both sides.

7.2 Implementation Planning

A detailed plan showing the activities that will occur during the first 12 months of implementation should be drawn up. As will be seen from the rest of this chapter, many activities take place during this period. It will probably be best to develop the plan on two levels—a high-level plan describing the major tasks to be carried out (of which there will probably be about 10), and another, which is much more detailed, showing the individual subtasks (of which there will probably be about 100). Table 7.1 shows an example of a high-level plan. Table 7.2 shows an extract from the more detailed plan. For many tasks it will be difficult to accurately estimate the starting date or duration, but this is not a reason for excluding them from the plan. Progress review is an activity that should also be included in the plan. As much information as possible should be included for major milestones. If external resources are to be used during this period, they too should be included in the plan. External resources used could include management consultants, software developers, and system vendor specialists.

The implementation plan needs to be defined and agreed to. The hierarchic level at which these activities are carried out will depend on the size of the company and the implementation effort required. The driving force for the plan should be the highest-level person who will have responsibility for the development and use of CAD/CAM. This could be the CAD/CAM director. Definition of the individual items of the plan could be the responsibility of the CAD/CAM manager, provided of course that this person has been appointed. It may be that the task force plays a major role in planning activities, since this should be the most knowledgeable group of people in the company. Even if they are not involved in developing the plan, their approval should be requested. Top management and middle management should also be required to sign off on the plan. Middle management involvement is particularly important, as it is often "their" people who will carry out

TABLE 7.1 Major High-Level First-Year Tasks

Develop plans for installation-related activities and other activities that will occur during the first year's use.
Carry out training of managers, users, support staff, and other parties.
Prepare purchase order/sign contracts. Fix delivery date.
Finalize site location and facility layout.
Prepare for system installation and acceptance.
Develop procedures/standards for system use, support, and management.
Install, test, and accept system.
Adapt system to company—conversions, macros, documentation, etc.
Use system. Communicate experience.
Monitor and review progress. Report progress.

TABLE 7.2 Detailed Low-Level Tasks Related to Facility Preparation

Develop detailed plans for facility-preparation–related tasks.
Identify potential sites.
Define detailed requirements (e.g., for power, space, environment control).
Select site.
Define detailed site and facility layout.
Build facility.
Order major systems (power, air conditioning, etc.). Order furniture and supplies. Define facility tests.
Receive and install systems, furniture, and supplies.
Test facility without CAD/CAM system.
Install CAD/CAM system.
Test facility with CAD/CAM system.

the planned activities or, at least, be affected by the plan. It is rarely a good idea to separate responsibility for preparation of a plan from responsibility for its implementation. If the CAD/CAM manager is to be held responsible for the success of CAD/CAM, then this person should have a major role in the planning process. Similarly, people who will take little or no responsibility for the implementation should play no more than minor roles in planning. A CAD/CAM manager who is not involved in the planning process may feel little commitment to the success of the plan and may consciously or subconsciously behave so as to modify its objectives.

One difficulty in developing the plan is that of inexperience. It must not be forgotten that CAD/CAM involves change—in individuals' jobs, in organization, in responsibilities, and in the way that information is used. These changes will affect the whole organization. There will be few people in the company who have experience planning for this type of changing, unknown environment. It may well be beneficial to request help from a more experienced source.

7.3 Preparing for CAD/CAM

There are many activities that must be carried out during the first year of implementation—installing the system, educating and training staff, developing procedures and standards, and so on. This section looks at all the activities apart from the physical installation of the system, which will be covered in the next section.

The first major activity concerns people. They need to learn about CAD/CAM and the way to use it. All types of people need to be made more aware of CAD/CAM and the benefits it can bring. During the first year, top management will want to learn more about the new technology it has invested in and the way in which it should be used to provide maximum benefits. Middle managers need to learn about the effect that CAD/CAM will have on the engineering and manufacturing activities for which they have responsibility. Middle managers of other functions for which CAD/CAM does not appear to have a major effect should also be educated. As time goes by it may be found that CAD/CAM does have an effect on areas, such as purchasing and marketing, that appear to be outside the mainstream engineering and manufacturing areas. The CAD/CAM support team needs to learn about system support (which will probably be relatively complex and unknown to them) and use (which will probably not be documented). Last but not least, the direct users of the system need to be trained to use it.

The question of who should be trained first is linked to the questions of which applications and which projects should be the first to be carried out with CAD/CAM. During the first year it is important that use of CAD/CAM appear successful. This is one of the most important factors (though clearly it should not conflict with longer-term objectives) when choosing how to start using CAD/CAM. A fairly small project that can be handled by well-proven functions of the system may be a good starting point. The first users should be people who have the basic skills to work on this particular project, who want to use CAD/CAM, who will learn quickly, and who will not give up quickly.

It will be necessary at some time (the sooner the better) to select a CAD/CAM manager and the CAD/CAM support team members. The profile of the CAD/CAM manager has been detailed in other chapters.

It is a very difficult job. The role of the CAD/CAM manager is key to the successful use of CAD/CAM. Once the CAD/CAM manager has been selected it should not be difficult to select the CAD/CAM support team members. The team members will need to be trained to operate the system, to maintain it, to optimize its performance, and to give assistance to users. They may also be trained so that they can train future users and encourage potential users to use the system.

It may be helpful to set up a CAD/CAM steering committee. The role of this committee will be to see that CAD/CAM meets user requirements. Its members will be representatives and managers of users. The CAD/CAM manager will probably be invited to participate in at least a part of each committee meeting. Figure 7.1 shows the position of the steering committee in the overall CAD/CAM organization. Some of the task force members may initially serve on the steering committee. As time goes by and CAD/CAM is introduced to new areas of the company, representatives of these areas will join the committee. In the event of major developments affecting CAD/CAM, the CAD/CAM director will find the steering committee to be a good source of user requirements.

Procedures have to be established so that people can work effec-

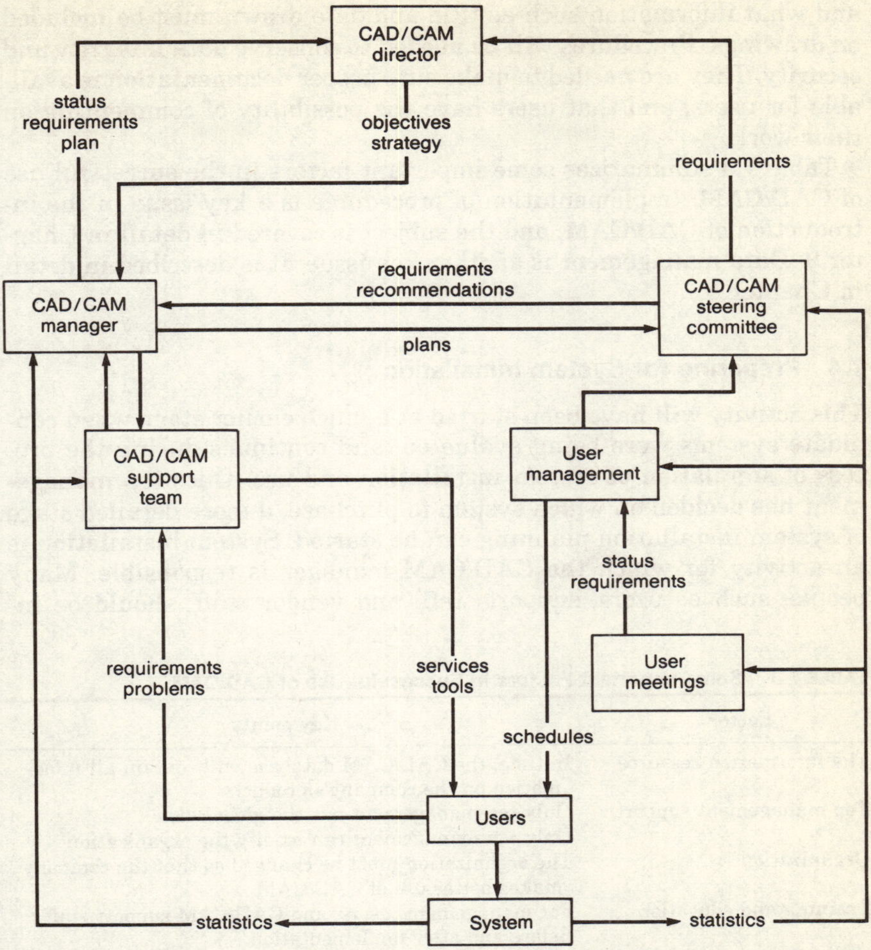

Figure 7.1 The position of the CAD/CAM steering committee.

tively in the new CAD/CAM environment. Procedures cover the complete range of use, operation, management, and development of CAD/CAM. They are needed for explaining how to build up a library of standard parts and how to use the library. They are needed to explain how to stop and start the CAD/CAM system, the screens, and the plotters. They will show how to manage models and drawings of products through the different stages of work: under review, released, and archived. Procedures will be needed to show how parameterized drawings can be created, modified, and used. They will show how drawings and models should be numbered, how drawing formats should be used, and what information such as title and date drawn must be included on drawings. Procedures will be needed to conserve data integrity and security. They are needed to make sure proper documentation is available for users, and that users have the possibility of commenting on their work.

Table 7.3 summarizes some important factors in the successful use of CAD/CAM. Implementation of procedures is a key issue in the introduction of CAD/CAM, and the subject is covered in detail in Chapter 9. Data management is another key issue. It is described in detail in Chapter 8.

7.4 Preparing for System Installation

This activity will have been started at a much earlier stage when candidate systems were being evaluated, and continues during the process of simulation of system installation and use. Once top management has decided on which system to purchase, a more detailed stage of system installation planning can be started. System installation is an activity for which the CAD/CAM manager is responsible. Many people, such as users, support staff, and vendor staff, should be in-

TABLE 7.3 Some Important Factors in Successful Use of CAD/CAM

Factor	Key points
The information resource	In time, the CAD/CAM database will contain all information on the company's products
Top management support	Only top management has the global view Only top management can modify the organization
Organization	The organization must be changed so that the company makes better use of CAD/CAM
Training and education	For management, users, and CAD/CAM support staff Before and after implementation Perhaps the major cost of CAD/CAM
Analysis of requirements	In the absence of a suitable analysis of company requirements, the wrong system may be chosen or the right system used in the wrong way
Focused applications	Decide which applications will gain most from CAD/CAM Concentrate on doing them well. When that is achieved, move on
The right CAD/CAM system	The modeler Data management Potential for interfaces
System support and operations	Develop suitable procedures Monitor and report
System development	Vendor-supplied developments Internal developments
Motivated users with good engineering skills	Train and support Develop career path

volved in the planning and installation process. Users should be involved to make sure that the final installation meets their requirements. The vendor will be consulted to take advantage of experience gained with other installations and for information on system requirements for power, space, and so on. A certain amount of this activity needs to be carried out before the contract is signed. This will cover, in particular, those tasks related to defining the costs of installation. The rest of the activity will be carried out after the contract is signed, when everyone is sure that the installation will go ahead.

Major tasks in this activity include selection of a suitable site and the detailed design of its layout. These will be very company-specific, depending on geographic layout, user location, system limitations, and other organizational factors. Apart from the layout of the basic system components (such as the computer, workstations, storage devices, and input/output devices), the layout of furniture and storage space for supplies and information must also be considered. The system components will be stored under different conditions depending on their environmental and security requirements. Material, such as disks and tapes, that is used for long-term archiving of information should be stored in danger-proof storage in a temperature- and humidity-controlled environment.

Some of the system equipment (such as the computer and storage devices) only needs to be accessed by the CAD/CAM support team. It should be installed in a controlled-access and controlled-environment room, which will probably have to be specially built or adapted for this purpose. Temperature and humidity should be continuously monitored and controlled in this room. A false floor will provide a convenient place for cabling and allow easy access to it. An air-filtration unit may be required. Special power sources or electrical equipment may be needed to protect equipment from sudden power supply changes. In addition to the equipment, the room should also include basic furniture that may be required for system operation, maintenance, and storage of a limited number of disks, tapes, and manuals. Some free space should be allowed for so that equipment can be easily dismantled for maintenance. More free space may be needed so that future system expansion will not require demolition of the facility.

Consideration must also be given to the peripherals (such as plotters) that will usually be operated by the support team but will occasionally be accessed by users. Again, the peripherals should be kept in a controlled-environment room, and in early stages it will probably be contiguous with the computer room. Apart from the peripherals, the room may also contain basic storage equipment (for drawings, tapes, manuals, and supplies).

The workstations should be in a quiet area well away from noisy computer equipment, such as printers and cooling fans. At initial installation time, though, it may be difficult to balance the need to separate the different types of equipment with the desire to centralize resources. There are good reasons for centralizing resources initially, even though in the long run they will most probably be distributed at user locations. Grouping resources is often cheaper, as it reduces duplication requirements and overhead costs, eases communication problems, and conveniently aids training, support, and management. Its major disadvantages—extra travel and separating users from their normal working environment—should not cause too many problems when the system is initially installed.

In addition to balancing the needs of centralization and distribution of resources, it will also be necessary to balance the need for physical security of information with that for free access to information. In areas where designs and drawings of new products are produced additional security may be needed. Similarly, access to information storage media such as tapes and disks may need to be restricted.

Even if the workstations are not centralized, they should at least be grouped together in clusters in the user's local environment. This will remove the travel problem and lessen the feeling that CAD/CAM belongs to a world that is completely separate from the traditional environment. At the same time, it allows users to maintain effective local communication while minimizing system maintenance and management requirements.

The workstation environment needs to be one in which users can work effectively and productively. They will not be able to do this if they are irritated by noise, heat, uncomfortable furniture, inappropriate working surfaces, lack of storage space, static, unsuitable lighting, and other distractions. The environment needs to be temperature- and humidity-controlled, and shielded from the noise of equipment and extraneous conversations. Screens need to be placed so that users do not suffer from strong reflections. It may be necessary to provide blinds for windows, as well as user-controllable lighting. The users should be able to adjust their screens and chairs to the most comfortable positions. A working surface for drawings and models and some storage space for the individual user should be associated with each workstation. Common storage space will be needed for manuals, documentation, drawings, models, and so on; which leads back to the topic of data security, which will have to be examined in detail. It may be necessary to provide complete privacy at some individual workstations, or for particular clusters. Access to workstations will probably require knowledge of a project-dependent password. Care will have to be taken in storing and archiving data. Access to the workstation area may be restricted to badge holders.

7.5 System Installation and Acceptance Testing

After the contract for system purchase has been defined, the CAD/CAM manager will know the expected delivery date for the system, and consequently will be able to plan for the tasks associated with installation and acceptance. It is advisable to check occasionally that there is no slippage in delivery date.

The CAD/CAM manager will be responsible for the activities of system installation and acceptance testing. They cover the time between the physical arrival of the system and its acceptance as a piece of equipment that can be used on an everyday basis. Many of the tasks associated with installation have been covered in the previous section. In the same way that those tasks were started well before system installation, the tasks associated with acceptance testing must also be started well before the system arrives. Although the vendor will carry out a standard series of tests to show that the system is working, it is advisable to carry out some extra tests that check those parts of the system that are most critical to its use in the company. Before the system arrives, some time should be set aside to define the necessary tests, and after installation, some time should also be set aside for them to be carried out. It is not a good idea for the future users of the system to carry out these tests unless they already have a deep knowledge of the system. Instead it will probably be best if a member of the support team with an understanding of the application requirements is given this task.

Physical receipt of the system should be acknowledged. In the presence of vendor staff, the equipment should be received, inspected, and, if necessary, stored. Apart from major equipment items, other equipment, spares, documentation, disks, and so on should also be formally received. The vendor can then go ahead and get the system running and carry out the standard operational checks.

Before formally accepting the system, the company-specific tests should be carried out so that before the final payment is made, the CAD/CAM staff is sure that the system does what it is expected to do. These tests will give company staff the first opportunity to get hands-on experience with "their" system. Throughout the duration of acceptance tests, detailed records should be kept of all actions so that in the unlikely event of problems occurring, an "audit trail" is available from which the vendor can reconstruct the problem. Hopefully there will be no problems, and the system can be formally accepted. Should there be problems, negotiations will have to take place between company and vendor managements to find a solution that is acceptable from both the technical and financial points of view.

7.6 Adapting the System to the Company

All companies are different and have different requirements, so it is not surprising that many of them find it necessary to adapt (or customize) the purchased CAD/CAM system to make it meet their particular requirements. Complete customization may take a long time (more than 1 year), and therefore will extend beyond the time frame examined here. However, there are many such tasks that will be completed in the first year, and others that will be started in the first year and completed later. The tasks to be carried out should have been identified and planned earlier. They should be carried out mainly in order of their priority from the viewpoint of overall company objectives. However, some visible early success should come from the adaptations, so it is not a good idea to only embark on lengthy tasks for which success is long term or uncertain.

Typical areas that may require customizing are macros and links to other systems. A *macro* is a set of several commonly used commands. Once it has been built it can be invoked with a single command, thus saving time and reducing the potential for errors. Since different companies use CAD/CAM differently, they will employ different sets of commands; therefore, the macros tend to be company-specific. Similarly the links to other systems, manual or computer-based, tend to be company-specific.

The system must work alongside other systems in the company. Typical areas where it may be necessary to provide interfaces are production planning and technical documentation.

The interface with production planning may be through the bill of material—a document that lists all the items required to make a product. The bill of material serves production by defining which items are to be purchased or manufactured, and when these actions and material purchase should occur. Engineering can generate the bill of material from the parts lists associated with the detailed description of a product. If care is not taken, engineering and production will not work according to a common bill of material. CAD/CAM offers an opportunity to rationalize the situation.

Engineering staff spend a significant amount of time working on text documents (such as change documents) and mixed text and graphics documents (such as maintenance manuals). Most CAD/CAM systems do not really address these areas, and the company may find it useful to investigate the possibility of introducing technical office automation to improve the productivity of these tasks. Another very company-specific subject is documentation. The system vendor will supply documentation showing how the system functions. However, users need to know how to use the system within the company environment, and the vendor documentation does not tell them this. The company must find out how to use CAD/CAM for its particular requirements, then document this knowledge and make it available to users.

A company-specific library of standard parts may need to be built up, and can be a key element in the search for savings of time and money. Some companies may want to build up a limited catalog of products that can be supplied on a magnetic medium to potential clients. Special programs that previously ran on other systems may have to be converted so that they run efficiently in the new environment.

7.7 Starting to Use the System

At this stage, the system should be running well, the first applications should have been selected, and people should have been assigned to this work. This may be the time for some concentrated training. Initially it may be best to separate the CAD/CAM trainees from staff carrying out manual work. The training course can be given in a compact and quiet location. System support will be easier because all the resources are grouped together. Although many benefits result from initially "centralizing" resources and users, this is not necessarily the long-term solution, since, in some cases, it can create a feeling of "us and them" and can hinder the integration of CAD/CAM into the everyday workings of the company.

The first few weeks of system use are often very difficult for the users who have had little previous experience of CAD/CAM and computers. All possible assistance should be given to them at this time. This may mean that the CAD/CAM support team may have to work 16 hours a day to keep up with them. Some of the users will be more than happy to work on the system and may also spend 16 hours a day learning how to use it. Before long it will probably be necessary to implement workstation control procedures and to think about introducing double-shift work or at least some form of flexible working hours. There is no universally applicable solution to the problems that arise from having fewer workstations than users. Some companies make users reserve time slots for workstation use. There are generally rules about the number of slots that can be reserved in a day and the number of consecutive slots that can be reserved. The rules can be set so that every user has the chance to get to a workstation at least once a day. Some users will not like the system because they have to give up a workstation when they are "warmed up." However, if the time slots are calculated judiciously, users should have enough time to do some useful work but not so much that they start doing things that would be better done away from an expensive workstation.

Flexible working hours can help to improve the availability of workstations. They can also help to improve the total use of the system—which will probably be to management's liking. There is a limit to the flexibility of working hours that white-collar workers have traditionally been prepared to accept, and typically this means that it is not possible to introduce a second shift. It is also questionable whether a double shift is useful, as it will greatly reduce communications. The solution that many companies have found is to operate an overlapping double shift. One shift may work from 6 to 2 and the other from 12 to 8. Figure 7.2 shows how the amount of productive time at the workstation can be increased by good management. The example is for a company with 4 workstations and 20 users.

During the initial stages of CAD/CAM use, it is important that the CAD/CAM manager keep in close contact with the users and listen to their experience—good and bad—with the system. The feedback is important—both to help resolve problems and to build up a base of good practice.

During the early stages of CAD/CAM use, many people will question what kind of work should be carried out with the system. Should easy problems or difficult problems be tackled? Should libraries of common parts be built up prior to starting complete designs? Should existing drawings be entered on the system? Should CAD/CAM be introduced on projects that are already under development, or should it be introduced on a completely new project? Of course, all these questions should have been resolved a long time ago, but they will nonetheless be asked again. They should have been resolved as a function of overall company objectives, so, for example, the question of whether existing drawings need to be entered on the system will depend on what use the company will make of these in the future. It may be that it is necessary to enter some drawings. The most important ones should be entered first, but before they are entered, they should be examined with an eye toward perhaps modifying them to be more suitable for future use in the CAD/CAM environment. If some parts have a strong family resemblance, it may be possible to parameterize some of their characteristics.

Once the users have learned the basics of system use, the roles of the CAD/CAM manager and the support team will begin to change. Instead of being mainly responsible for system selection and installation, their major role will become one of providing an efficient day-to-day service for both the short and long term.

Scenario 1. Single shift. No workstation management	
8:30 a.m.	CAD/CAM support staff switch system on. Users arrive on site, wake up, collect thoughts, drink coffee.
9:00 a.m.	Users attend project meetings.
10:00 a.m.	Project meetings end. Users demotivated, exit for fresh air, drink coffee.
10:30 a.m.	Users ready to use screens. All 20 users arrive simultaneously at the four screens. Discussions and violence break out
11:00 a.m.	Turmoil dies down. The four users who won a screen find they have not prepared all the data they need. They go off to get it.
11:30 a.m.	The four users work productively at the screen.
12:15 a.m.	The users leave their screens so that they will arrive at the canteen before it closes.
12:30 a.m.	All 20 users at lunch.
1:30 p.m.	All 20 users return from lunch. Discussions held with designers and managers.
2:30 p.m.	Users ready to use workstations. All 20 users arrive simultaneously at the four screens. One screen is being used by CAD/CAM support staff for development work, another is undergoing preventive maintenance.
3:00 p.m.	Turmoil dies down. Two users have won workstations. They get down to work.
5:30 p.m.	CAD/CAM support team switch system off.
Useful working time: 4 × 45 min + 2 × 2½ hours = 8 hours	

Scenario 2. Two shifts. Workstation scheduling	
6:00 a.m.	First shift arrives. Four users at screens.
8:00 a.m.	Four different users take over.
10:00 a.m.	Second changeover. Four users at screens.
11:00 a.m.	Second shift arrives. Four users at screens, five at lunch, four in meetings.
12:00 a.m.	All 20 users present. Four users at screens, five at lunch, eight in meetings.
1:00 p.m.	All users present. Four users at screens, five at lunch, nine in meetings.
2:00 p.m.	All users present. Four users at screens, five at lunch, five in meetings.
3:00 p.m.	First shift over. Four users at screens.
4:00 p.m.	Four users at screens.
6:00 p.m.	Four users at screens.
8:00 p.m.	Second shift over.
Useful working time: 14 × 4 hours = 56 hours	

Figure 7.2 The effects of workstation management and shifts.

7.8 The Relationship with the Vendor

The vendor should be seen as a potentially very helpful partner for the process of implementing CAD/CAM in the company. Unfortunately, such a partnership does not always develop. Sometimes this is because vendor staff have oversold the system, so after installation it does not live up to expectations. Sometimes it is because the company has not really understood the potential of CAD/CAM or the resources that must be committed if it is to be used successfully. This state of affairs is unfortunate, especially during early stages when company staff are rarely sufficiently knowledgeable to be completely independent and can benefit from all the assistance that the vendor can offer. If they do not really believe the vendor's word, they are unlikely to benefit as much as possible.

Even after use of the system has gone beyond the teething stage, it is preferable to have a good relationship with the vendor. Through other customers, the vendor will have wide experience of the ways that the system is used and can pass on useful information. Since few companies will want to get involved in major developments of the system, the vendor will be the major source of improvements and extensions to system hardware and software. Similarly, the vendor will probably be the major source of maintenance, unless this is contracted out to a third party.

Provided that the relationship with the vendor is good, a continuous flow of useful advice, developments, and contacts should ensue. The vendor will be happy to put the company in contact with other users with similar applications, and joint projects may develop.

User groups, which bring together members of the various companies using a particular system, are associated with most systems. Meetings of user groups provide a forum for users to learn from each other, to compare notes, to discuss and hopefully to solve common problems, and perhaps to agree to jointly request the vendor to make certain improvements or modifications to the system. Although user groups are usually completely independent of the vendor, there is generally a good communication channel between the vendor and the user group.

7.9 Monitoring and Reviewing Progress

Unless this task is recognized to be important and included in the implementation plan, it will probably be forgotten and ignored once things really start to get moving. There will be so many other important and necessary activities leading to "real" progress that no one will have the time to check what progress really is being made. Activity cannot always be equated to progress, especially when progress has clearly been defined as relating to the company's objectives. In many cases, activity in the CAD/CAM area is close to panic and has little to do with achieving objectives. The purpose of monitoring and reviewing progress is not to identify and punish the guilty, but to identify as soon as possible discrepancies with the plan and to take the necessary corrective action. It may be that it is only after the system has been put into use that it becomes apparent that the original requirements study was not sufficiently wide-ranging or that the volume of system use was underestimated.

Different people in the company will be interested in the results of the progress review for different reasons. Top management will be looking to see what kind of return on investment is being achieved. Hopefully no one will have led them to believe that major benefits will appear in the first year—since they rarely do. The CAD/CAM manager will be looking to see what problems have occurred and how they can be solved. If the introduction of CAD/CAM has been successful, people from outside the current group of CAD/CAM users will be wondering whether it can be applied in their areas. Current users of the system will be interested in a quantitative evaluation of the work that they have carried out and in any suggestions that are made for improvement.

A review at the end of the first year's use of CAD/CAM should not be costly either in time or in money. It may be suitable to get someone from outside the company to carry out the review. This should help to ensure that it is unbiased and does not use up the valuable time of company staff who could be carrying out other, product-related work. Alternatively, the review could be carried out by task force members. Being familiar with the original objectives for use of CAD/CAM, they should be able to recognize fairly readily whether these have been met.

The review will involve looking at the real results from use of the system, analyzing the periodic reports that have been produced by the CAD/CAM manager and project managers, interviewing management and users, watching people using the system, evaluating the amount and effectiveness of training, and so on. It may be that some of the information is not available—this in itself is a meaningful finding since it may mean that reporting procedures are being ignored or that correct training procedures are not being followed.

7.10 Typical First-Year Problems

The first year of implementing and using CAD/CAM is fraught with danger. The CAD/CAM manager will soon find that there is risk associated with every CAD/CAM opportunity, and that people who should be firm supporters of CAD/CAM can just as easily be highly destructive. The CAD/CAM manager will look back over the system selection process and reminisce about the ease of that essentially theoretical task. The real problems arise when theory has to be put into practice, people have to carry out new tasks, and organizational change (rather than talk of organizational change) is necessary.

Table 7.4 shows some of the problems that often appear in the first

TABLE 7.4 Some Problems that Often Appear in the First Year's Use

Problem areas	Problems
The CAD/CAM system	The users don't like it Response times are too long The vendor goes out of business It's underutilized
Top management	Immediate payback expected No foresight or understanding No commitment or support Don't change the organization
Middle management	CAD/CAM conflicts with their goals Empire syndrome CAD/CAM is too risky for real projects Afraid of loss of power
Users	Afraid of loss of job Don't want to be computer operators Once trained, may leave No methodology to use system
Implementation	Start on a high, finish on a low Planners not responsible The money is cut off No leader, no champion
Information	The system can't handle all the information People don't reuse information, they re-create it Data is not secure Interdepartmental barriers prevent information flow
System support	No procedures in place No money to pay for support Support staff leave No records kept
System development	Difficulty of developing in absence of standards Vendor does not support the system Internal developments are not maintained 18-month waiting list for developments

year of CAD/CAM use. It can be seen that they stem from a variety of sources. The CAD/CAM manager must be alert to the possibility of ill winds blowing from many quarters. The problems may be caused by top management withdrawing support from the previously agreed plan. Sometimes they will be due to middle managers unable to handle the traumatic changes that will inevitably accompany the introduction of CAD/CAM. In other cases it will be the users who, faced with the difficulties of working with a new system and new techniques, do not succeed. Sometimes the problems are directly due to malfunction of the system hardware or software, or to the inability of the CAD/CAM manager to provide suitable system support and development. Often, problems arise because people believe that selecting a system represents 95 percent of the activities associated with using

CAD/CAM. Once the system is selected they sit back, believing that successful use of CAD/CAM will follow automatically. Of course, it does not. The selection of the system only accounts for a few percent of the total activities. Another problem may arise from a lack of discipline. In the absence of suitable procedures, people will use the system as well as they can, but will invariably make mistakes. Data will be destroyed, projects will overrun their budgets, or it will not be possible to find previously created data. CAD/CAM could then lead to a reduction in productivity, rather than the hoped-for improvement.

Forewarned is forearmed, and the CAD/CAM manager who is aware of the problems that may occur can take action to prevent them, and ensure that the objectives of implementation of CAD/CAM are met.

Chapter

8

CAD/CAM Data Management

8.1 File-Based CAD/CAM Data Management

During the first 20 years of the development and use of CAD/CAM, most data was stored in files directly controlled by the computer's operating system. In an environment where there were only a few users and all the files were created and used on the same computer, initially this did not cause too many problems. However, as time went by and more and more files were created, it became difficult for the users to remember exactly where their data was, and even more difficult for them to follow their colleagues' developments. Each drawing could be stored in a separate file; each three-dimensional model might be spread over 10 or 20 files. Before long, there would be several thousand files in existence, ranging in size from a kilobyte to many megabytes. Disk space was too expensive for storing this amount of data, so some files had to be stored (or archived) on magnetic tape.

If a few users trying to keep track of their own data had such problems, what of a large company trying to use computer-based engineering information as effectively as possible? Their files are probably spread over many computers using different operating systems. If the computers are from several vendors, there is no simple method for sharing files and data. The company has spent 1 or 2 years building up what it believes to be a large database of engineering information from which it will be able to go on and obtain the real benefits of CAD/CAM. However, a few small disasters then occur because manufacturing uses unreleased versions of data, data slips through the review process without receiving suitable authorizations, projects are finished unnecessarily late because managers lose track of the status of drawings, and reports come in of a defect in a year-old product for which no one can work out the as-built configuration. Engineering management then realizes that it is not enough to have CAD/CAM and a sea of data, but that the whole issue of creating and using engineering information in a computer environment needs to be addressed. New procedures have to be introduced for a range of activities, such as release control, engineering change control, and configuration and project management. If the level of detail is expanded to the contents of the data files, the problem is seen to be even worse. Within a data file, vendors store information in different ways. They may use different geometric models of a part, but even if they use the same model, they may store data elements differently. Thus one vendor may store a circle as its center and radius, whereas another vendor may store it as three points on its circumference. One vendor may physically store the representation in the order: x-coordinate of center, y-coordinate of center, radius, whereas another might store it in the order: radius, x-coordinate, y-coordinate. In this type of environment it becomes difficult for systems to read, let alone change, the data in another system. It will not be easy for a user to find out which flanges are available on CAD/CAM when the CAD/CAM information is spread over half a dozen different systems.

The above description may seem a little extreme, especially to those who have managed file-based systems successfully. In a single-vendor single-computer environment a lot can be achieved with the features of some standard operating systems. For example, the different parts of the file name can be assigned special meanings. One part can represent a project name, another part can show the release status, and a third part can show the version number. Rules concerning use of the design layers available in the system can be defined so that information of a particular type can be accessed without simultaneously accessing information that is not required. A library of frequently used data can be implemented. The password structure and privilege rights controlled by the operating system can be tailored to restrict data access to authorized users. Data can be archived regularly and stored in a secure and environmentally controlled area. However, even such a well-organized environment will become inefficient as the amount of CAD/CAM data increases and an attempt is made to make better use of the information content of the data.

8.2 Problems with Data in the File Environment

Engineering information is difficult to manage in the typical multivendor, multisystem, multiapplication, cross-functional, multilocation environment. It is difficult for all sorts of reasons—data storage, version control, release control, configuration control, project control, and so on. In such a distributed environment it is difficult to implement centralized control. No two companies have exactly the same engineering information requirements, so a company cannot expect to buy a standard solution. Each company will have to tailor its own configuration to fit its engineering information requirements. Unless this is planned for, the opposite will happen, and the company will end up fitting its information to the constraints of the computer system.

Another problem arises because the data storage and management capabilities of successive versions of a CAD/CAM system from a given vendor can be incompatible. The vendor upgrades the system to offer better functionality and a richer information content, but in doing so can create the situation where the earlier version cannot make use of all the data in the later version and the later version may be limited in its use of data created under the earlier version. From the information point of view, this situation will continue as vendors strive to enrich the description of the product model. Thus the information a company stores on its CAD/CAM system today could require "renovation" in 5 years if it is to be of any real use.

CAD/CAM hardware has problems that parallel the ones related to the evolution of CAD/CAM software. The CAD/CAM information generated today by a company, such as an aircraft manufacturer, may have to be recalled in 20 years. It is unlikely that the CAD/CAM hardware used to generate that data will be in existence then (unless it is in a museum), so it will be difficult to re-create the exact environment.

Over the 20-year period, the company will generate enormous volumes of information. As the amount of information concerning product definition increases, individual users may create gigabytes of data per year. This alone will create a management problem unless storage technologies evolve. What type of data should be stored for future use? Should it be three-dimensional models or two-dimensional drawings? The two-dimensional drawings may meet today's manufacturing requirements, but the three-dimensional model may be what is needed in the future.

International standards, which are discussed in more detail in Section 8.5, could be of help in deciding how to store the increasing amount of data. However, they have tended to lag many years behind the needs of users and the technological advances of vendors.

Even if the above problems could be solved, there would be the problem of the thousands of data files that are created. Engineers are interested in objects not data files. Conceptually, there is a big difference between the two. The contents of a data file only have real meaning to the program that writes the file, i.e., data is not independent of the program. From an engineering point of view, information should be independent of all programs. File-based applications are expensive and time-consuming to change, and the easier (though probably incorrect) alternative may be to develop a new program with a new data structure. Files contain a mixture of data representing graphic, textual, and numeric information—unless the format is known exactly, the file cannot be read. The cost of developing and maintaining programs that need to access data in files in systems developed by different vendors to cover different functional areas is prohibitive. Instead, it may be decided to include some manual intervention with consequent loss of time and introduction of errors. With so many files in place, redundant data will abound. Its introduction is a waste of effort, and invariably leads to multiple representations (or misrepresentations) of the same physical entities. With files spread over many computers, users may find that they need several terminals on their desk to access all their data.

In the above example, it has been assumed that the problems are limited to an individual company. However, most companies have to transfer data to and from other organizations, such as vendors, customers, subcontractors, and government agencies. Invariably this introduces more problems, because these organizations have different computers, systems, release procedures, and so on.

Looking to the future, it is expected that knowledge-based systems should be able to help in the decision processes associated with engineering. This will not occur until it becomes possible to freely access data without the individual user knowing the details of all the files, systems, and computers in the configuration. As the industrial environment becomes more competitive, companies will switch their emphasis from reducing direct costs to reducing indirect costs. Among the major ways in which engineering's indirect and administrative costs can be reduced are (1) improving the flow and use of engineering information and (2) improving access to it.

There is a large variation in the kinds of engineering information that need to be managed. Although the particular information requirements of a specific company will be unique, there will be similarities between companies in the same industrial sector. Typically, there will be information that describes the product, describes the process, supports the product activities (such as standards), and supports the process activities (such as facility drawings and machine maintenance procedures). Some of the information, such as standards and standardized parts, will be common to many activities of the company. Other information will be product- or project-specific.

Engineering companies already have manually operated systems to manage data on "hard" media such as paper, mylar, and microfilm. With the introduction of computer-aided engineering systems, though, an increasing amount of data is produced and stored electronically on disks and tapes. A new data management system will be needed to manage this information. Initially, an attempt will probably be made to manage this data manually, but the inefficiencies that result make a computer-based engineering data management system a necessity.

8.3 Requirements of an Engineering Data Management System

Before defining the requirements of an engineering data management system, it is necessary to consider just what type of data will be managed by such a system and how it will be used. Most engineers will tend to think that it will manage the type of data they work with. However, most engineers only work with a small subset of the total engineering data. A real engineering data management system would not be so restrictive. Instead, it should be able to handle any, and all, data created in the engineering process. There will be geometric data in the form of drawings or CAD/CAM-produced models, machine-tool control programs, process recipes and set points, maintenance documentation, and specifications and change orders. There will also be information that is less easy to visualize; for example, the criteria that an engineer used when deciding how to go about a particular engineering task. The data management system should manage product information throughout the product life cycle, e.g., maintenance information may still be required 30 years after the product was designed.

The objectives of the data management system will appear different to different people in the company. Many of those in daily contact with large quantities of difficult-to-manage data will be looking for a system that will efficiently store and retrieve data. They will need some archiving facilities, and they will appreciate effective configuration management and version control. They will welcome a reduction in the number of errors and the amount of rework. At another level, others will view the system as a tool that helps ensure the reuse of existing data. Still others will want the system to reduce engineering costs. These objectives are not necessarily contradictory, and the same system could meet all these requirements. It is worth understanding, though, that different people will be looking for different advantages from the introduction of such a system.

One of the difficulties in developing an engineering data management system is that there is such a wide range of users and such a variety of data. The data can be in the forms of graphics, text, mathematical formulas, and numbers. Sets of data come in many different sizes, formats, and types. Engineers may want the same system to manage the letter "L" representing a parametric length, a twenty-first order polynomial, a straight line, and a subroutine of a program.

The users of the system will be carrying out all sorts of functions in the company. Some will be creating data, others will modify it, while others will only want to view it. Some of the users will be "head-in-the-clouds" designers; others will be "feet-on-the-ground" shop-floor workers. The system will have to be of use not only in engineering and production but also in marketing and purchasing. Most of the users will really be using the data; others will be managing the engineering process. Managers will need to define data access rights for users on a per-project basis, and perhaps even on a per-part basis. They will want to know the status of developments and of projects, and to use the system for managing the review cycle and producing project management reports. The range of users and activities could hardly be wider.

The data itself has many different structures. At the lowest level it will represent letters, digits, and points—all of which are of individual interest to particular users. At the other extreme it may represent a complete product such as an aircraft. The user who wants to interact with an "aircraft" does not want to be bothered by all the levels of detail down to individual coordinates on the fuselage. The system has to be able to handle the "objects" that the user wants to work with and the structure of the objects. The aircraft is an object of interest to some users, but the wing is an object of interest to other users, while the wing flap may be of interest to yet another group. The data management system has to be able to handle objects at different levels of the structure so that the users can handle the objects at their particular interest level. Although data has to take its place in the overall structure, it also needs to have a local significance. Individual users will want to develop their own sets of data which may correspond, for example, to a project for a new aircraft or for a particular part of an aircraft. The data management system must be capable of connecting individual sets of data, on a per-project, per-object, and per-function basis. The system must also be able to associate different representations of the same object, such as its geometry, its specifications, and its physical characteristics.

Different users of the engineering data management system will want to see a given object in different ways. Salespeople will not want to see the same "views" of a car as structural engineers do. They may also want to see different structural relationships within the data. Sometimes it will be necessary to identify a particular part of a known car. This will probably be a hierarchic structure—i.e., by knowing the maker, model, year, and version of the car, the user will be able to identify a particular part, such as a wheel. Another user may want to look at all the wheels ever used by the company. In this case the hierarchic technique used in the previous case would be much too slow.

The engineering data management system needs to be able to recognize and maintain a variety of relationships between data elements and sets. In addition to the types of relationships mentioned above, there are also those expressed in configuration and version control; for example, if a new version of a product is put on the market, the system should be able to show which parts of the associated maintenance manual need to be updated.

A variety of other requirements must be met. The data may be physically distributed over several sites, yet it must be available at all sites. Not all the data may be computer-based; some may be on paper. The data may be on systems that represent data in different ways. The user does not want to worry about such technical details, so automatic (and correct) data translation between systems may be needed. Several people may want to work on the same data at the same time, so the system may have to decide which people have the right to make modifications and how other users should be informed of those modifications. Engineering management may want the system to play an engineering procedure support role, helping users to carry out their work in accordance with the company's engineering rules and preventing them from making costly mistakes.

Since the engineering information will be spread over computers from several vendors, data management also has to address the questions of data recovery (i.e., what happens if a computer crashes) and data distribution (i.e., transferring data between heterogeneous environments). The data management system should be able to handle information queries coming from all levels of users throughout the company.

Within the system, data should be written so that special interfaces need not be developed in order for all programs to make use of the data. The data needs to be sufficiently accessible that new programs that make use of the store of knowledge managed by the system can be developed at low cost. The data management system interface needs to be such that, in time, expert systems can interact with the database.

There is the danger of course that such a powerful system would have an extremely slow response time unless it was "tuned" to meet a well-defined, fixed set of requirements. However, engineering data management systems will undergo rapid changes in the foreseeable future, and a system designed to meet a fixed set of requirements today will be out of date within a few years. Engineering data management systems need to be designed for a fast response to a wide range of requirements and a rapidly changing environment.

The term "database" does not imply that all the information must physically reside in one place. It was mentioned earlier that some information is common to the company, some is specific to a particular function, and some flows through several functions. An analysis of current and expected use and communication of information should be completed prior to selecting the engineering data management system. From this analysis it may become apparent that data should be physically centralized. Alternatively, it may be better to physically distribute the data while maintaining centralized control.

8.4 Remember the Production Department

There is a tendency to think that engineering information only concerns the engineering department. However, as has been mentioned several times, this is not so. Engineering information is used by people throughout the company. Marketing, personnel, sales, and finance and administration all make use of engineering information. Perhaps the most important users, though, are those in areas directly related to production. These people will have skills different from those in the engineering department, and the representations of the product that they work with differ from those that engineers work with.

The engineering data management system must take into account the requirements of both the production planners and the shop-floor workers. Production personnel may be at a completely different physical site or in a different company from the engineering personnel. They work with a mixture of textual, numeric, and graphic information that is different from the mixture used in engineering. They may require more concrete, less abstract representations of information than those used in engineering. They may have time-related constraints, such as the definition and scheduling of product mixes, that engineering does not have. Data associated with an aerodynamic model of an aircraft will be of little interest to the workers responsible for the production of an individual fuselage panel or a composite fin.

In process industries, recipes and set points for use on the shop floor will be generated by engineers and stored in the engineering database. In discrete industries, machine-tool control programs, inspection programs, and product information needs to be transferred to the shop floor. In the future, this transfer may be electronic, with much of the data being available on low-cost shop-floor terminals rather than on paper.

8.5 Data Exchange

The more one looks at the use of engineering information, the more apparent becomes the need to exchange data. Data has to be exchanged between people within the same function, people with different functions in the same company, and companies interacting with each other. In time, companies will also be faced with the problem of exchanging data between different versions of their CAD/CAM systems. Suppliers will want to transfer CAD/CAM-based catalogs of products to potential clients.

The information that must be produced before a product can be manufactured can be split into three classes. There is data that defines (1) the product itself (traditionally the result of design engineering), (2) the manufacturing process (traditionally the result of manufacturing engineering), and (3) when the product is to be manufactured (traditionally the result of production planning). Item 3 is generally regarded as being outside the area of CAD/CAM.

Manufacturing process data is in a "final state." When it is exchanged, it is usually in the form in which it will be used and will not be further modified. However, product definition data, on the other hand, is rarely in its final state when it is transferred. It is generally being transferred to another design engineering function (where it will be modified or where inferences will be drawn from it to produce additional data) or to a manufacturing engineering function (where it will be used as the basis for defining the manufacturing process). If, as a result of the data transfer, the final state of the data is not exactly the same as the initial state, then problems will occur. The data exchange requirement of most companies is a program that will read data from one of their CAD/CAM systems (call it system A) and write it to the database of another CAD/CAM system (call it system B) such that system B then has exactly the same information as system A. If necessary, the data should then be exchanged between system B and a third system such that if it were then exchanged back to system A the original and new versions of the data on system A would be identical.

The problem for many companies is that such exchanges tend to be physically difficult and often result in information corruption. The exchange is actually made up of two parts—a transfer and a conversion. The transfer of data between databases of different systems running on different computers using different operating systems is made difficult by the lack of standardization in the realms of database interfaces, operating systems, and communications. Efforts are being made to implement acceptable standards such as the International Standards Organization (ISO) Open System Interconnect (OSI) seven-level standard and the associated MAP and TOP protocols.

The transfer problem is not specific to CAD/CAM. It is met by all users who need to transfer information between different computer systems. However, the conversion of product definition data is more specific to CAD/CAM. There are three levels of product definition: a graphic definition, a geometric description, and a complete product description. Graphic data exchange is not specific to CAD/CAM, and it occurs in many areas where the "picture" on one graphics screen needs to be displayed on a screen of a different make. Unfortunately, the data representation of a picture on one screen does not necessarily produce the same picture on another type of screen since terminal manufacturers have different ways of defining pictures and interpreting data. Attempts to overcome this problem have been made by developing standards such as CORE and ISO's Graphical Kernel System (GKS) that are intended to render the presentation of graphics information device independent. However, graphics technology advances fast, and no sooner is a standard introduced than it seems to become out of date. Currently, standardization efforts in the area of graphics are leading to GKS-3D and Programmers Hierarchical Interactive Graphics System (PHIGS).

If standardization of graphics, where there is a limited number of basic entities (such as points, lines, and characters), has been difficult, it can be expected that standardization of geometric models, which have a much wider range of basic entities, has been even more difficult. There are four major classes of geometric models (two-dimensional, three-dimensional wireframe, three-dimensional surface, and three-dimensional solid). There are subclasses of these classes; for example, solid modeling can be approached by the constructive solid geometry (CSG) method or the boundary representation (B-Rep) method. Within subclasses there are a variety of different representations of the same physical entity. A complex surface may be represented by Coon's surfaces, Bezier surfaces, B-spline surfaces, or rational B-spline surfaces. CAD/CAM systems from different manufacturers use a different subset of entities; thus, when an attempt is made to convert a geometric entity from system A to system B, system B may not even recognize the existence of that entity.

The need to exchange product definition data between different CAD/CAM systems is so great that significant international effort has been expended in the attempt to develop a standard. The basic requirement of users is a way to read data out of their CAD/CAM system (system A) and to write exactly the same information into the database of another system (system B). One way to do this is to develop a program that reads the data from system A, translates it to system B format, and writes it into system B's database. Translators of this type, known as *direct translators*, have been developed (Figure 8.1). They generally work well for the specific pair of systems for which they are written. When modifications are made to the data representations of the systems involved, the direct translators have to be modified. This is not a problem if only a small number of systems are involved, but for the general case of n systems, a total of $n(n - 1)$ direct

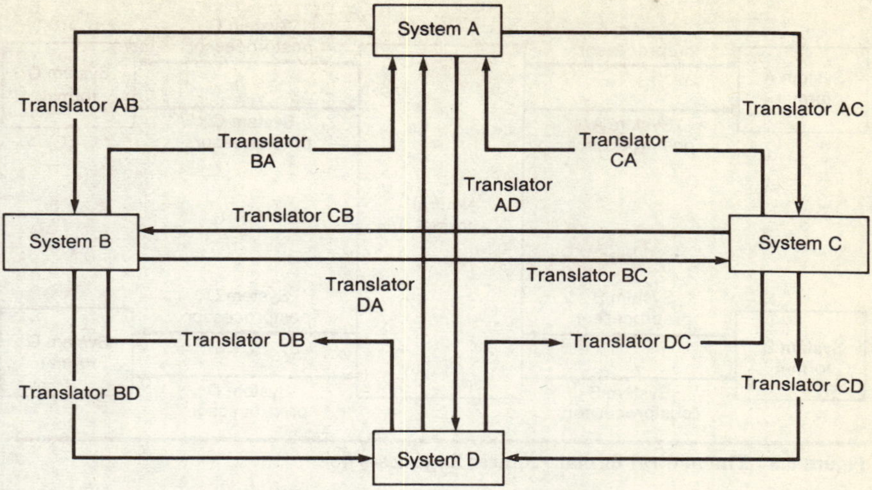

Figure 8.1 Direct translation requires $n(n-1)$ translators.

translators are needed. If n is 50, then the total number of direct translators required becomes very high (2450).

Efforts toward standardization have taken a different direction—that of the intermediate neutral format. In this method, each system has a program called a *preprocessor* which can convert data from its own format to the neutral format and another program called a *postprocessor* which can convert data from the neutral format to its own specific format. Thus in the case of the transfer from system A to system B, the preprocessor of system A translates data from its particular format into the neutral format and the postprocessor of system B translates this data from neutral format to its own specific format (Figures 8.2 and 8.3). With such a method, in the general case of n systems, a total of $2n$ programs is required—a significant reduction compared to the number of direct translators needed when n is large. The success of such a method is highly dependent on the number of entities that are defined in the neutral format. Unfortunately, many of the standards proposed have not been sufficiently rich in neutral format entities to allow all users to exchange all the necessary information.

Figure 8.2 The principle of the neutral format file.

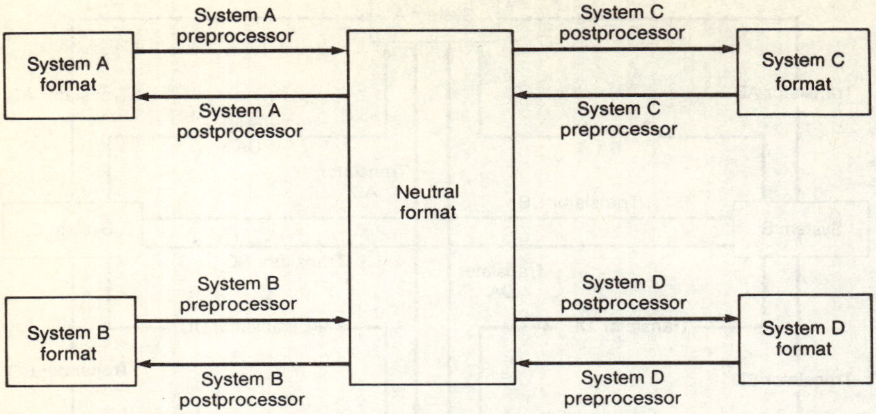

Figure 8.3 The neutral format requires $2n$ processors.

The Initial Graphics Exchange Specification (IGES) was the first standard proposed. It is mainly used to exchange the geometric entities of drawings and wireframe three-dimensional models. It became an ANSI standard in 1981. Many users found it insufficient and further work was carried out to define a better standard. In the United States, the USAF ICAM Product Definition Data Interface (PDDI) activity investigated the need to include more than geometric data in the standard. As a result, a new standard, Product Data Exchange Specification (PDES) has been proposed by the United States. It includes nongeometric information such as material properties, form features, topologic relationships, attributes, tolerances, and administrative information (such as release dates). In Germany, the VDA-FS standard was adopted in 1984. In France, Standard d'Echange et de Transfert (SET) was adopted as a standard in 1985. Current ISO efforts are directed toward producing a common international standard. Previously known as Standard for the Exchange of Product Model Data (STEP), it is the responsibility of ISO committee TC 184-SC4; a first draft of its specification is expected in 1988.

It has been mentioned in previous chapters that some CAD/CAM systems are more suited to particular application areas. In the same way, product modeling neutral formats will tend to be application-oriented. The basic entities that make up a PCB are different from those of an aircraft wing from both the geometric and logical points of view.

8.6 The Value of the Engineering Database

The objective of CAD/CAM is to improve the flow, quality, and use of engineering information. The engineering database is at the heart of CAD/CAM. When defining how engineering data will be managed, the CAD/CAM manager needs to look much further than bytes and files, and address the question of how the engineering database management system will help the company meet its CAD/CAM goals. The intention of the system should not be to manage a walled-in store of engineering data, but to create an environment in which users throughout the company have rapid, secure, and correct access to the data they require.

A good engineering data management system cannot be implemented in the absence of a good understanding of the use and flow of information within the company—and in particular within engineering. Without such an understanding it is probable that data will be redundant and transmitted unnecessarily and inefficiently. When implementing CAD/CAM there is always the danger that in the rush to become productive, the necessary time will not be taken to select the best way to use information in the CAD/CAM environment. Instead, data use will be automated in a way that mimics the manual environment, which may have once been suitable, but may no longer be. Almost certainly this will not be the best solution.

In order to identify the requirements for efficient use of information (Figure 8.4), it is necessary to investigate and understand the way that (1) engineering information is used in engineering, in the rest of the company, and by external organizations, and (2) the way that engineers use information created in other parts of the company.

Within the engineering department there are clearly information flows between different tasks. Data created in design engineering is used in manufacturing engineering tasks such as process planning and part programming. Producibility information generated by manufacturing engineers is transmitted to design engineers. As the investigation into the use of information continues, many examples will be found of departments making use of "common" data: production planners use parts lists; process plans are used on the shop floor; quality-control information is fed back to engineering.

There is an information package associated with the product life cycle. The package starts off small—perhaps it only contains a few lines of text describing the required characteristics of the product—and gets bigger as engineers define the product's detailed description. More information is added to describe how the product should be made, how the particular product was made, and what happened to it during its life.

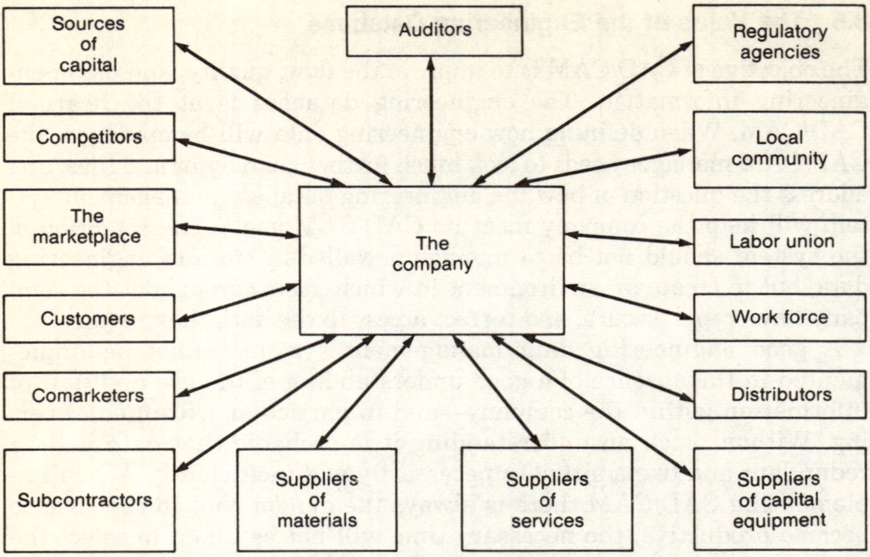

Figure 8.4 Information flows and the company environment.

The availability at the required time of the required product information is a key element in successful use of CAD/CAM. It will be only too easy for the CAD/CAM manager to forget this in the search for a suitable engineering database management system. Vendors of such systems tend to stress the functionality of their systems, not the way in which they are integrated into a company's overall operations; yet this is the aim of the CAD/CAM manager.

In addition to pure "data management" functions, an engineering data management system (EDMS) can also be used to help manage the engineering process. In the same way that a process plan can be set up to describe how a part is to be manufactured, an engineering process plan can be set up to describe the engineering tasks that are required to develop, for example, the design of a part. Once the project manager has entered the plan in the EDMS, the system can then control the process—making files available to the right people, informing people when they are required to do something, controlling access to data, making sure that the correct release and revision procedures are followed, and so on.

8.7 Introducing the Database Management System

The data produced by most CAD/CAM systems is stored in files. From the point of view of the CAD/CAM program developer, this is a good solution since the files can be organized to optimize program performance. From the point of view of the engineering organization running many programs, it is not such a good solution. Modification to data elements results in the need to modify programs. Data in the files produced by one program cannot be easily accessed by other programs. Transfer of data will first require up-to-date and detailed knowledge of the position, format, and meaning of data in another file. The physical transfer may occur through a set of interfaces and require changes in format and type.

The traditional file system is said to be program-oriented since the data cannot be accessed without knowledge of the program that produced it. A database system is data-oriented. It contains all necessary information on the data so that a given data set can be accessed without knowledge of the program that produced it.

Database management systems are used widely for commercial and financial applications. In such applications the structure of particular types of data is generally fairly standard. The employee record in such a database might contain 20 pieces (fields) of information such as name, address, telephone number, salary, and so on. The information will be in alphanumeric form. The employee record will be the same length for all employees. In engineering applications, though, things are more complex, and for this reason, engineering database management systems are much more difficult to develop. Compared to the simplicity of the employee record, the record describing a product is very complex. For different products, different pieces of information will be stored. They will be of different lengths. Some will be in the form of variable-length alphanumeric strings, some will represent mathematical equations, and some will be in the form of tables of numeric values. Transactions in financial applications, such as updating an account, last a few seconds. An engineering transaction, such as updating a three-dimensional model, may take several days. However, the advantages of the database management system are such that in time, systems that meet the requirements of most engineering organizations will be developed.

The database itself serves as a common repository for engineering data that can be accessed by many engineering users and programs. The database management system manages the data so that this task no longer has to be carried out by each individual program. Since there is a common management system, a common language can be used to access the data, and it becomes possible to find and reformat data automatically as instructed by the user.

In a file-based system, growth occurs mainly through an increase in the number of files. The database system allows for an increase in the range of data held without modifying existing programs or introducing redundant data.

The major elements of a database management system are the database, data models, data management functions, and query programs. The data models describe the organization of relationships between data elements. Some of the most frequently used data models are described in the next section.

A data definition language (DDL) is used to define data elements. A data dictionary (DD) maintains data definitions and the rules by which data can be accessed. The DD knows, for example, where a data element is stored, how it is defined, and the corresponding access and retrieval methods. The DD contains the schema and subschemas (logical structure) of the database that describe the way in which a particular program or user looks at data.

A data manipulation language (DML) allows a computer program to access the data managed by the database management system. A query language allows a user, for example, an engineer sitting at a screen, to access data directly, independent of any other program. Database management systems offer a wide variety of benefits when compared to file-based systems: a common repository of data, elimination of redundant data, access control, and security. All programs have access to the same set of data, which in turn is independent of individual programs so programs and their modifications can be introduced without disturbing the data environment of other programs. For the casual user who does not have programming knowledge, the query language offers an effective and easy way to access data.

Against these benefits must be weighed the cost of introducing such a system and the overhead it represents in everyday use. Its introduction requires examination (and probably modification) of all existing programs.

8.8 Database Architecture

This section describes the architectures of the database. The three major types of models are the hierarchic model (Figure 8.5), the network model (Figure 8.6), and the relational model (Figure 8.7).

In the *hierarchic method*, each entity is represented by a record whose fields contain the value of its attributes. Records are related by a hierarchic, or tree-structured, parent/child relationship. The "top" entity in the structure does not have a parent record. All other entities in the structure have only one parent but can have many children. Only one-to-many relationships between data entities can be defined in the hierarchic model, and pointers are used to show the logical links between data entities. The model is suitable for some engineer-

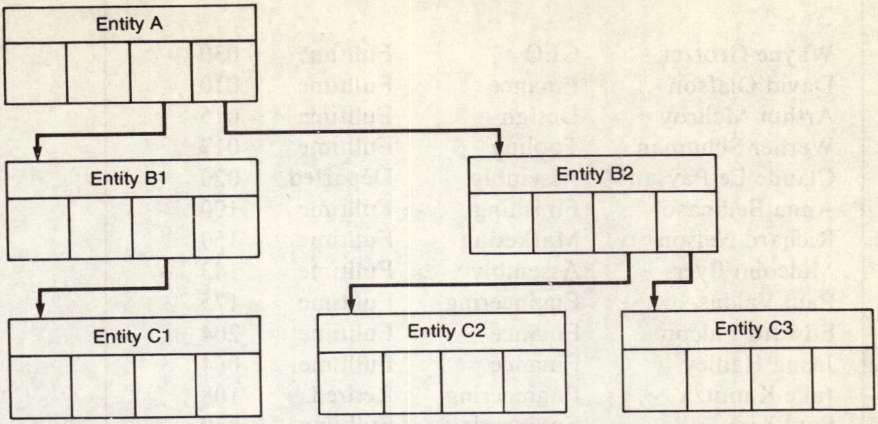

Figure 8.5 The hierarchical data model.

ing applications, for example, those involving simple hierarchic structures such as engineering assemblies. However, there are many engineering relationships that are not purely hierarchic. In these cases, the representation of relationships can become very complex and considerable redundancy of data may occur.

In the *network model*, each entity is represented by a record whose fields contain the value of its attributes. Arbitrary relationships are allowed between data entities. A given entity can have any num-

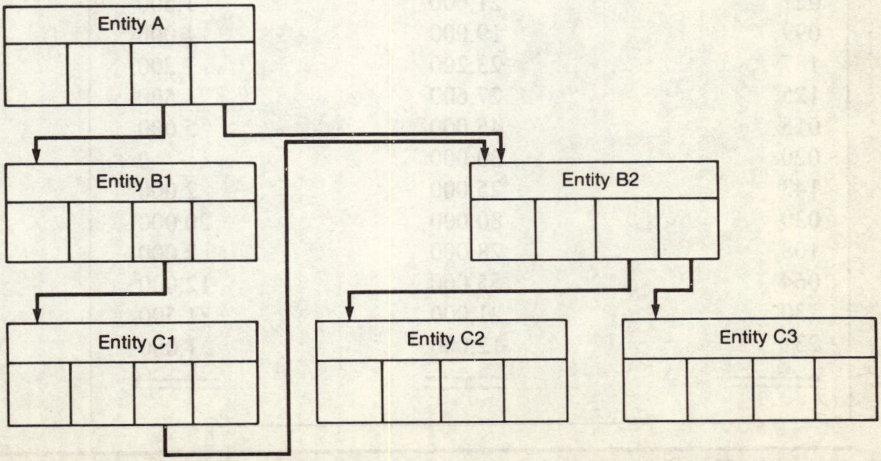

Figure 8.6 The network data model.

Table Employees

Name	Department	Status	Number
Wayne Grotzer	CEO	Fulltime	030
David Olafson	Finance	Fulltime	010
Arthur McIlroy	Design	Fulltime	015
Werner Schuman	Tooling	Fulltime	017
Claude Le Paysan	Assembly	Departed	020
Anna Bellinaso	Finishing	Fulltime	100
Richard Nelson	Marketing	Fulltime	150
Malcolm Byers	Assembly	Fulltime	143
Paul Valdas	Engineering	Fulltime	175
Edward Falcon	Finance	Fulltime	204
Jasna Hadley	Finance	Fulltime	064
Jake Kanutza	Engineering	Retired	108
Paul Kim	Engineering	Fulltime	230
Edward Ludd	CADCAM	Part-time	231
================	===========	=========	====

Table Employee Salary

Number	Salary	Bonus
010	60,000	10,000
150	30,600	2,000
204	35,000	3,000
036	26,500	2,000
027	21,000	1,500
099	19,000	1,000
187	23,200	1,200
125	27,600	1,500
015	45,000	5,000
020	30,000	0
143	25,000	2,000
030	80,000	20,000
108	28,000	2,000
064	55,000	12,000
230	21,000	1,500
231	12,000	1,000
=======	======	=======

Figure 8.7 The relational data model.

ber of parents and any number of children. It is possible to define many-to-many relationships, and pointers are used to show the logical links between data entities. For many engineering applications a network model will perform better than a hierarchic model. The many-to-many relationships improve access speed through the database. They also overcome problems of redundant data.

In the *relational model*, data entities are represented in two-dimensional tables known as relations. Each horizontal row of the table may be seen as a record that represents the attributes of an entity. Each vertical column contains the occurrences of a given attribute for the entities.

In the hierarchic and network models, pointers are the links between database entities. In the relational database, the links between data entities are provided by the attributes. The adjective "relational" comes from the mathematics of sets, which offers excellent techniques for handling data in tabular form. Another advantage of the relational data model is that it offers easy modification of the database. The absence of pointers of the type found in hierarchic and network models makes addition and deletion of relations and entities much simpler. The relational database overcomes many of the problems of the file-oriented environment. The programs that access such a system are independent of both the logical database design and its physical implementation. Data independence is achieved.

8.9 Metadatabase Systems

Database management systems are used widely for commercial and financial applications, but, for various reasons (some of which have been mentioned above), their use in engineering is not as extensive. Nevertheless, many engineering departments have had to solve the problems arising from the proliferation of engineering files. One solution that has been found is the metadatabase.

A metadatabase system is a database management system that contains characteristic information concerning each of a set of files. In the simplest case, the metadatabase system is not aware of the contents of the files. Such a system might be limited to managing access to the files, in which case it would contain the basic information such as file names, version numbers, and access rights. It could have the capability to scramble file names to force all users to pass through the query language of such a system. A more advanced system could associate attributes with the information stored in each file. The next step could involve the introduction of configuration management for files accessed through the system. Then, event-driven task management could be added. The result, although it lacks the advantages of a true engineering database management system, offers limited but useful data management and project control functions.

To illustrate the difference between a complete engineering database management system (EDBMS) and an engineering metadatabase management system, each can be compared to the operation of an automated library. In the complete EDBMS, the contents of the books represent the database and a catalog represents the data dictionary. From the catalog, the system can determine which book or group of books has the information required by a user. The information is then retrieved and transmitted to the user. In the metadatabase system the catalog is the database. The system identifies which books contain the information and then transmits complete copies of these books to the user. It could be said that the basic functions of the metadatabase are to catalog files and manage access to them. These basic functions can be extended by the introduction of more user-defined information about each file. The status and history of each file can be maintained, relationships can be set up with other files, and attributes that describe some of the characteristics of the file can be included. If the system contains definitions of the expected file-related events (such as change of status, sign-off, and release) prior to the start of a project, the system can assist project management.

8.10 Planning for Engineering Data Management

As has been seen, database management systems are data-oriented, whereas file-based data management systems are program-oriented. In the file-based environment, planning is generally concentrated on identification of required functions, with data requirements being of secondary importance. In the database environment, the definition of data requirements is extremely important, and the planning process becomes much more data-oriented. The first step of the planning process is to develop a model describing the use and flow of information throughout the company and within its business environment. It draws a picture of the current state of data usage throughout the company. It could be argued that this is unnecessary since what is required is a picture of the future state of data usage. However, experience shows that very few people are capable of drawing the picture of the future without fully understanding the current one. Experience also shows that very few people and, perhaps more important, very few managers have any real understanding of current data usage. Although the modeling process will take a lot of time, and consequently cost a lot of money, it is the necessary first step.

Once the current picture of data usage has been obtained, it—along with the strategic objectives of the enterprise—will serve as the basis for defining the future data usage picture. With this definition in hand, logical data structure requirements can be developed and related to the major functions of the company. Data characteristics such as expected volumes and necessary response times can be calculated. Once the company has completely defined its requirements, a particular database management system can be selected.

The USAF ICAM project was mentioned previously in connection with PDDI. The ICAM project also led to an information modeling methodology known as the ICAM definition system (IDEF). Three IDEF models are used to describe the company; IDEF (0) describes the functional structure, IDEF (1) describes the data, and IDEF (2) describes the flow of materials and information. Computer-based systems based on IDEF methodology have been developed, because in view of the amount of data involved, it is very difficult to model a company's use of information without them.

Information will become an increasingly important asset that a company must use as well as possible to gain competitive advantage. The engineering data management system will play an important part in this process. The person responsible for managing the company's engineering information and systems will have an important—and interesting—role.

Chapter

9

CAD/CAM Procedures

After installation, a CAD/CAM system should quickly become an integral part of the company and show a return on the investment made. For this to occur, the use of CAD/CAM must be clearly defined and its role in the design and manufacturing process unambiguously stated. Procedures define this role and the way in which CAD/CAM is linked to and affects other aspects of the company.

9.1 Introduction

Procedures are formalized working practices that have been agreed upon, reviewed, and accepted by management. The purpose of CAD/CAM procedures is to help ensure that the best practice is identified and then followed by all parties. They are similar to any other company standard and will not by their mere existence have any effect. They must be adopted and supported by management and they must become part of the fabric of the company.

Each company is different, with its own strengths and weaknesses. The environment of each company is different. The most effective application of CAD/CAM will therefore vary among companies. This difference will be reflected in a company's CAD/CAM strategies and procedures. The sample procedures described in this chapter cannot therefore be automatically applied to all applications in all companies.

The introduction of CAD/CAM should have a major impact on the way that a company carries out its business. Achieving the available benefits will inevitably require a number of changes, some perhaps quite radical. These changes should be discussed and agreed upon by the staff that is to use the system, either directly or indirectly. Existing boundaries between departments and disciplines will change, and new skills will become increasingly important. In this environment of change, formal procedures are needed to ensure that all parties are aware of their responsibilities and their relationships with the rest of the company. Further change can be expected to occur. As a result, all procedures, especially those for CAD/CAM, will require updating to take advantage of experience and the opportunities provided by improved technology.

As the use of CAD/CAM develops, the company's investment in its database increases. Procedures control and protect this investment, and it is important that they enhance rather than detract from CAD/CAM's usefulness. It should be noted that after the system has been installed for over 2 years, the investment in design data may be worth more than the cost of the system, maintenance, and training put together. If the data has not been created in a structured manner, carefully maintained, and stored for later access, then the investment will not provide the expected return. Procedures are a means for achieving this return on the company's investment in CAD/CAM.

9.2 Procedures May Seem Tedious, but They Are Necessary

It might be thought that the only thing more boring than reading a procedure is writing one. However, reading a whole chapter about procedures is a serious contender. Yet a whole chapter is necessary because procedures are so important. Preparing and reading procedures may be tedious, but working without them—and having informal working methods of dubious quality that change from user to user and department to department—can be even more time-consuming. Running a CAD/CAM system without procedures is similar to having a highway system without a highway code and traffic signs. Such a system will work while there are only a few users, each responsible for their own activity, but as the number of users increases and the need to share data and work together grows, the problems start to arise. Procedures should provide the ground rules and framework for coordinating activity at several different sources.

In the absence of procedures, how can the CAD/CAM manager respond to a user who has lost work because of a known system problem? In the absence of procedures no one will know whether the user knew of the fault and, if so, had written documentation showing how to avoid it. Procedures will not solve such problems, but they may provide the information to stop them from occurring. Procedures should guide and advise the user, highlighting possible problem areas and suggesting ways around them.

Small installations can frequently get by, for a time, without formal procedures. The users are likely to be self-selecting: The staff most interested and keen to work with CAD/CAM are the ones that will use it the most. They will probably be well versed in the system and have a good idea of what they are doing. They will probably use informally defined working methods based on their own individual experience of the installed system. These methods will be limited by their knowledge of the system and will, in some instances, be based more on supposition than on a true understanding of the system's functionality. In such cases, the use of CAD/CAM and its interface with other departments is unlikely to be in line with company strategy, and overall company requirements will almost certainly take a back seat to local expediency.

As the use of CAD/CAM expands, so does the scope of the problems and the impact on the company. Inappropriate interfaces and working methods that do not integrate CAD/CAM into other areas of the business will only magnify difficulties and detract from business performance. The development of a well-conceived set of procedures at this stage is an effective way of recovering the situation. Their preparation and adoption is probably one of the only ways to prevent the continuation of bad practices. If they are developed with the cooperation and involvement of users, they can be seen as a means for simplifying the use of CAD/CAM and making life easier for all concerned.

CAD/CAM procedures provide the formal framework for using the system and define its interface with the rest of the company. They therefore provide a reference for all staff who may come into contact with CAD/CAM and help ensure that it is consistently applied throughout the company. They will simplify the introduction of new users and should be included in the training program.

CAD/CAM procedures are a management tool; they define how the installation should be operated and formalize relationships internally and externally. Properly implemented and updated procedures can help ensure that basic errors are not made and that as problems arise they are solved and the information passed to all users. They do not solve problems, but provide a vehicle for avoiding them or, at the very least, dealing with difficulties in a consistent and controlled manner.

The extent and scope of procedures will depend upon the installed system and its desired application. Nevertheless, all CAD/CAM procedures must interface with existing standards and procedures, both formal and informal.

9.3 Scope of CAD/CAM Procedures

Procedures are needed to address three distinct areas that will be addressed in the next three sections: (1) design department procedures, (2) user interface procedures, and (3) system procedures.

There should be no need for formal procedures on the factory floor, but the use of CAD/CAM output there will need to be controlled. The data should be presented in a form suitable for direct use, without any other need than automatic reformatting. It is important that any problems found be fed back without delay to the design department to ensure that problems are not unnecessarily repeated.

9.4 Design Department Procedures

Design department user procedures should specify how engineering design work is carried out with the CAD/CAM system and define the interface with any manual methods. They should be general documents describing how the department is organized and how CAD/CAM work is controlled. Managers, supervisors, and users responsible for work that makes use of CAD/CAM will be the main users of these documents. The following procedures are required at a minimum.

Planning and initiation procedure
Data creation, update, and development procedure
Data checking, sign-off, and release procedure
Data change control procedure
Standard data creation and update procedure
Data transmission and reception procedure

Planning and initiation procedure

CAD/CAM activities should be planned in the same way as any other design activity. Due allowance for productivity differences compared to manual methods must be made. Training and system constraints must be taken into account.

Scope The steps required to plan and define how CAD/CAM will be applied to a given project or work area define the scope of this procedure.

Content The definition of how CAD/CAM will be applied needs to be established, as well as its scope and place in the program of work. Once defined, this information should be published as a formal CAD/CAM plan, a "live" document that will control and direct the work.

Checklist A good procedure to adhere to is as follows.

1. Check specifications and customer/project requirements. Do they need modifying to make the most of CAD/CAM?
2. Consider where the limited CAD/CAM resource can be applied with most benefit.
3. Identify any new procedures, training, software, or hardware needed for the defined work.
4. Review the current standard data and, if necessary, program the production of new information to meet the production schedule. This will include reviewing
   a. Drawing frames
   b. Library parts
   c. Menus
   d. Programs
   e. Macros
   f. Standard drawings and notes
5. Identify all CAD/CAM deliverables and their content.
6. Identify key CAD/CAM milestones in the work program. These will be different from the milestones used with manual methods and may include items such as the completion of training, preparation of software, and perhaps commissioning of new hardware.
7. Prepare a CAD/CAM plan and set up monitoring and feedback processes to enable progress and system effectiveness to be established.
8. Issue the plan and work to it.

Data creation, update, and development procedure

For three-dimensional modeling systems the extent of modeling and the different roles and uses for drawings and the model should be clearly stated. The model will normally be used to develop and prove the design. Drawings will be created from the model solely to transfer information to manufacturing and external third parties.

Scope The scope of this procedure includes all stages in the preparation of data from whatever source, with particular reference to the key stages of its development.

Content This procedure will define how the system shall be used and controlled by the engineering design facility to prepare and develop the data. It should start from the initial concept and continue through to the finished detail design transmitted to manufacturing.

Modeling checklist

1. Prepare model in block form to prove the concept.
2. Interface with analysis programs as appropriate, transferring data automatically whenever possible to speed up response times and reduce transcription errors.
3. Prove the model, possibly breaking it down into lower-level models to develop the design in greater detail.
4. Check the design model, including the CAD/CAM aspects.
5. Review the design model and return it for rework or further definition as necessary. Reviews should be carried out on the model information. (Formal drawings complete with annotation and dimensions should not be produced at this stage, even though there may be a strong lobby for them. The model contains the definition of the design. Formal drawings will have to be revised once the model has been updated in line with the review. So why create drawings at this stage?)
6. Once the design is complete, checked, approved, and released, then drawings, parts lists, and NC tapes can be produced from the model.

Drawing checklist

1. Select frame size and drafting standards.
2. If presenting model information, prepare views at correct scales.
3. Develop the drawing, annotate, and add dimensions.
4. Check the drawing and parts list, including the CAD/CAM aspects.

Data checking, sign-off, and release procedure

The ability of people to accept computerized output as correct, even when it flies in the face of their knowledge and experience, should not be underrated. The majority of data checks will be identical to those required for manual designs and should cover the engineering content. The additional information that must be verified for CAD/CAM output is that which pertains to its format on the system.

Scope This procedure defines the stages in the sign-off and release of all CAD/CAM data.

Content This procedure includes all the steps, in detail, necessary to check the design information. Some of the steps may appear pedantic, but careful checking ensures data quality and helps the system to become accepted throughout the company.

Checklist

1. Model or drawing name
2. Layers
3. Model or drawing structure
4. Use of standard data
5. Format

Data change control procedure

The fact that CAD/CAM data can be easily modified must not detract from the necessity for a formal change control process. The special importance of such control for CAD/CAM is that although any change to a three-dimensional model may be relatively simple, a large number of derived drawings, listings, and NC tapes—as well as output to linked systems such as MRP—could be affected. If this derived information is not updated and reissued consistently, the manufacturing process will suffer.

Scope This procedure details the control of change to all released CAD/CAM data from any source.

Content The method of reviewing, accepting, and implementing change to CAD/CAM data.

Checklist

1. Review change, and establish its impact on CAD/CAM data.
2. Estimate the project and financial implications.
3. Approve execution of change.
4. Change data at the highest level, progressively increasing the level of detail.
5. Identify all affected released documents, tapes, and transmitted data files that require modification.
6. Schedule and perform the change to all derived data.
7. Release the changes.

Standard data creation and update procedure

Scope The scope of this procedure is the creation and update of all standard CAD/CAM data, which includes two-dimensional symbols, drawing frames, common notes, and three-dimensional models of standard items such as valves, pumps, etc.

Content This procedure should describe how CAD/CAM standard data is defined, specified, and organized into different groups. The procedure must ensure that the standard data, especially the definitions of bought-out items and standard assemblies, fully reflect the company's engineering requirements and not merely system convenience. Rigorous checking and verification should be specified to ensure that both the CAD/CAM definition and the engineering content are correct.

Checklist

1. Check that the requirement cannot be met by existing standard data
2. Verify the engineering requirement: is it general or just project-specific?
3. Create the item.
4. Check the engineering content.
5. Check the CAD/CAM data, including the layering, data extract, interference volume, etc.
6. Update the standard library and inform all users.

Data transmission and reception procedure

Scope The scope of this procedure is the transfer of all data from or to the CAD/CAM system.

Content This procedure should cover the steps necessary to define and prove a transfer route between CAD/CAM and another system. The aim of the transfer could be to perform analysis, to update an external data base, to make use of third party data, or to provide the data for NC tape preparation.

Checklist

1. Define purpose of transfer and the required response time.
2. Establish scope of data.
3. Establish the most effective route, e.g., magnetic tape, floppy disk, modem, or a local area network.
4. Specify hardware and software.
5. Install link.
6. Perform checks with real data.
7. Prepare any procedures, including the specification of data naming, formatting, and checking.

The above topics may be covered by a single document or a series of related procedures. These areas need to be defined and controlled regardless of the type of system or its capabilities. If the CAD/CAM system is being used for three-dimensional modeling (either solids or wireframe) and drawings or machining data are being derived directly from the three-dimensional model, the control of the interface between the two-dimensional and three-dimensional domains and any nongraphic database is of prime importance. It is when defining such procedures that experience of CAD/CAM and its application to design is most useful.

9.5 User Interface Procedures

Procedures are required to define and describe the company's CAD/CAM user interface and assist all users, both casual and experienced, to gain the most benefit from CAD/CAM. These procedures, called *user guides*, should not duplicate the vendors' user manuals, but instead should show in detail how CAD/CAM should be used to achieve defined production objectives, such as the preparation of an electrical schematic drawing. The vendors' manuals generally concentrate on describing system commands and features, not their application.

A major ingredient of the recipe for high user productivity is good-quality user guides, supported by an effective user interface with software tuned to meet the company's production requirements. A CAD/CAM system computer is capable of repeating instructions and stringing together production commands. This capability enables the company to tune the software to meet specialized requirements. For the full benefits of CAD/CAM to be achieved, all such software improvements and new facilities must be transmitted to the users through controlled documents, i.e., user guides, which detail any nonstandard software in the context of real production work.

A feedback loop should be incorporated to allow hands-on users to identify enhancements for formal review by management and the system support staff. The result of this review should be fed back to the users to close the loop. The importance of allowing the hands-on user to influence the way that the system is developed and applied should not be underestimated, since it is they who are at the "coal face" and have the greatest knowledge of the way the system is currently being used.

Scope There should be one user guide for each major area of work undertaken on the CAD/CAM system. These areas include creating symbols, developing three-dimensional models, preparing two-dimensional models, and preparing NC tapes. Each user guide should include any special instructions and all the necessary guidance required to perform the defined task.

Checklist

1. Logging on and off
2. File naming
3. Symbol or figure library
4. Menu
5. Drawing frame
6. Layering
7. Structured material take-off lists and parts lists

9.6 System Procedures

In common with all computers, CAD/CAM systems must be controlled, supported, and maintained by well-conceived procedures if they are to perform effectively. The procedures will be specific to the system and, for the most part, their use should be restricted to the system support staff. The following are required at a minimum.

Naming convention procedure
Back-up procedure
Archive procedure
Vendor interface procedure
Enhancements procedure

CAD/CAM output procedure
Security procedure
Disaster procedure

Naming convention procedure

All reference to CAD/CAM data by the system is made through names. If names are not chosen in accordance with some agreed convention, a large amount of information will be created that cannot be effectively used or referenced by any system user other than the originator. The importance of an appropriate naming convention, established at the outset, cannot be too highly stressed. Renaming a large amount of existing CAD/CAM data because the initial convention was not comprehensive or failed to consider all relevant aspects is both wasteful and likely to cause errors and loss of data.

Scope The scope of this procedure is the convention that covers all CAD/CAM data from any source.

Content The convention, which may well be an appendix to another document, should define a structure and a means by which a meaningful name can be assigned to any CAD/CAM data.

Checklist

1. Models
2. Drawings
3. Material take-off files
4. Parts lists
5. Drawing frames
6. Symbols
7. IGES files
8. Macros
9. Program source code
10. Temporary files

Back-up procedure

All data should be backed up on an alternative device to protect against system malfunction or catastrophic failure. The usual medium is magnetic tape, and it is recommended that all data that has been modified during the day be backed up that day. All data should be backed up at not less than two weekly intervals. (Magnetic tape is considerably cheaper than rework.) The restoration of backed-up data must be carefully controlled, since this will often be unfinished work, part way through the development of the design. Re-creating lost work and checking where the data has been used for reference must be carefully carried out. The restoration of standard data need not be a problem if naming and database conventions have been carefully designed in the first place. The importance of giving each new or revised item of standard data a new name becomes apparent when the restoration of backups and archived data is considered in detail.

Scope This procedure covers the daily backing up of all CAD/CAM data.

Content This procedure should detail how backups are taken and restored. It is recommended that for all but the most sophisticated systems, which control the whole process automatically, a program be written to ensure that the correct data is backed up and that the information is available on disk.

Checklist

1. Back up all data changed in the last 24 hours, and update the disk reference.
2. Verify the data as it is dumped to the tape.
3. Ensure that data is thoroughly checked after being installed from a back-up copy.

Archive procedure

Data should be archived whenever it is either complete or at a defined stage required for later reference or record purposes. Magnetic tape is the normal medium for archiving data. Two copies should always be made of any data archived on magnetic tape. The medium is not perfect, and it is possible to return for information after only a matter of weeks and find that it cannot be restored. One copy of the archive data should be kept in a fireproof safe or off site.

The ability to access and search the complete set of archived tape records on disk is very useful. As the volume of CAD/CAM data expands this facility becomes increasingly important.

Scope This procedure covers the archiving of all CAD/CAM data, including models, drawings, symbols, macros, special software, and IGES files.

Content This procedure should define how data for archiving is labeled, detail the steps required in making the tapes (referring to vendor documentation as necessary), and describe how archived data is controlled and managed.

Checklist

1. Mark data as ready for archiving.
2. Dump to two magnetic tapes. Verify the data as it is transferred, updating the disk record.
3. Read both magnetic tapes and list them.
4. Remove the archived data from the disk.
5. Place one tape in a fireproof safe or off site.

Vendor interface procedure

The interface with the vendor should be carefully controlled. It is advisable to define a single point of contact for all system malfunctions, both hardware and software, to ensure that the vendor has a consistent and reasonably knowledgeable contact person. This will also ensure that new users do not call the vendor for "problems" that are neither repeatable nor likely to be due to a system malfunction. Throughout the life of the CAD/CAM system a number of problems will arise, some due to system failures and inadequacies, but many due to incorrect preparation and the misuse of existing data.

Wherever possible the system support staff should ensure that frequently required, critical repetitive steps that can be standardized are handled by macros or programs. The aim should always be to make it difficult for users to go wrong.

The procedure should include a means of communicating a serious problem within the company to ensure that management is aware of the difficulty and that the importance of the problem is emphasized to the vendor.

There should be a single person or body in the company that approves all future enhancements or new equipment from any vendor. This is especially important in large companies where there are a large number of different functional areas with varying needs that require coordination. This should not stop appropriate staff from reviewing the market to see how their individual requirements can be met, and it should help to ensure that compatible systems are chosen.

Scope This procedure covers all contact with CAD/CAM vendors.

Content There should be two main sections. The first should deal with controlling the contact with the vendor of existing equipment.

The second should define the steps necessary to prove, coordinate, and approve a requirement for CAD/CAM resources from any vendor and define how installation should take place.

Checklist

1. Schedule preventive maintenance visits.
2. Track progress of critical problems and bugs.

Enhancements procedure

Enhancements will be required throughout the life of the CAD/CAM installation. In general, they should be user-driven and -specified to meet well-defined requirements that provide a real business benefit. It is only too easy to pursue CAD/CAM technology for its own sake without looking at the broader business picture and the benefits that can be realized. Staff members with systems responsibility will obviously have the most knowledge of the CAD/CAM system's capabilities and the available options, but it must be the users that define requirements and their priorities. It should be remembered that the majority of the users will not be "computer literate" before they start to use CAD/CAM. Since most systems are based on providing a large range of options for creating and manipulating graphic data, it is very easy for users to get lost in the maze of options and techniques available and lose sight of the main task—engineering.

Scope This procedure covers the identification, review, and control of any enhancement to the CAD/CAM system, including both hardware and software.

Contents The procedure should describe how all enhancements are reviewed, evaluated, and implemented. For software developments, this should include the processes of defining requirements, preparing functional specifications, delivering the software within budget, and programming with proper project controls. For vendor-supplied hardware and software, the procedure should detail how upgrades are tested, accepted, and commissioned.

CAD/CAM output procedure

The quality of output from a CAD/CAM system is the same whatever the stage of the design. If a designer "sketches" some ideas on the system, the plot quality and presentation will be the same as that previously obtained from a tracing. In the manual process there is a single master document defining each part of the product. With CAD/CAM the item is defined by a computerized drawing and/or model which can be readily copied and modified by any user with access rights and used for plots that, at first glance, may be indistinguishable from the original data. It is therefore vitally important that all output be controlled and its status clearly indicated.

Scope This procedure covers the provision of all CAD/CAM output.

Content This procedure should contain the detailed steps required to produce plots, NC tapes, and magnetic tapes. The interface with other procedures controlling the use and checking of CAD/CAM output should be clearly identified.

Checklist

1. If the request is for a plot on film or an NC tape, is the data flag-identified to the system as complete and checked?
2. Check the plot for obvious errors before returning to the user, e.g., pen ran dry halfway through, or all text missing, etc.
3. Read NC tapes back into the system to check their content before they drive any machine.

Security procedure

CAD/CAM data residing on disk can be copied onto tape and/or transmitted down a telephone line very simply and quickly. Once transferred to another system, it can be copied and manipulated to suit the recipient. The security of confidential data is therefore of prime importance.

Scope This procedure should specify any specific security requirements for CAD/CAM data and equipment.

Content This procedure should describe how CAD/CAM data is to be secured and how physical access to modems, tape drives, and disk drives is to be restricted. It should describe the levels of protection necessary for all types of data from macros to models of sensitive or confidential items.

Disaster recovery procedure

As the CAD/CAM system becomes more important to the company, it becomes necessary to protect against loss of the system and to ensure that work can continue after a disaster. The method of controlling this recovery should be defined before the event, not as part of the disaster itself. The effect of, say, a fire should be considered in the light of other preparations that have been made throughout the company. It is hardly cost-effective to ensure that a standby CAD/CAM system is available for use with the data secured off site if the most likely disaster would destroy all the reference drawings, specifications, and other paperwork necessary to complete the design task.

9.7 A Framework for Procedures

To ensure that all procedures are created in a consistent and correct manner, with consultation between all relevant parties, the method of preparing CAD/CAM procedures should be documented. It should define how procedures are initiated, developed, and controlled and could be considered a "procedure for procedures." It should also provide an introduction to the set of procedures. CAD/CAM procedures can usually be more clearly and easily prepared as flowcharts, rather than as the more usual narrative documents. An example is shown in Figures 9.1 and 9.2. It consists of two facing

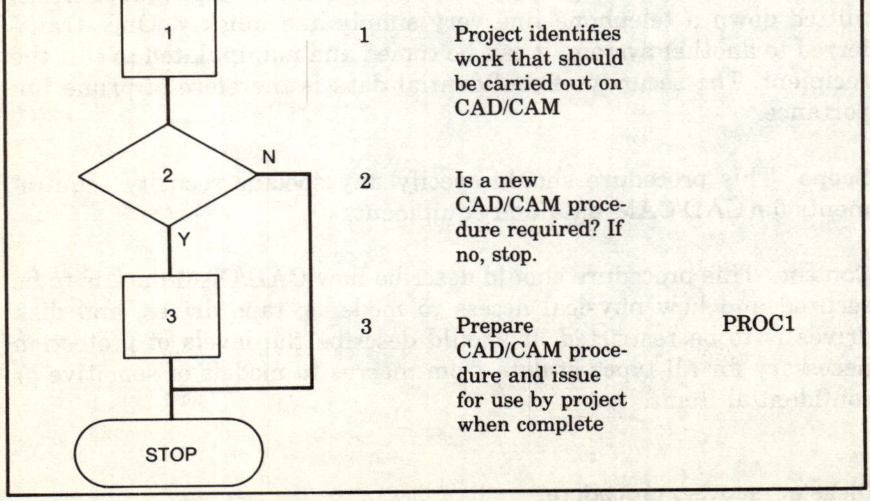

Figure 9.1 CAD/CAM procedure flowchart.

Activity	CAD/CAM manager	Project manager	Procedure writer	Notes
1	Advise	Initiate		Should be a joint activity that involves both the project team and the CAD/CAM manager
2	Advise	Decide	Advise	
3	Advise		Execute	Shall be carried out in accordance with the "Procedure for Procedures," PROC1

Figure 9.2 CAD/CAM procedure tasks.

pages: one describing the activity, the other defining responsibilities. The use of a flowchart simplifies the presentation of a procedure and helps to clarify the sequence of activities. It is easier to read than a text-based description, particularly when the logic offers many choices.

Procedure for procedures

Scope The procedure should encompass the initiation, development, and control of all CAD/CAM procedures.

Content A "procedure for procedures" should define the content and format of all controlled documents. The stages in a procedure's development should be specified and formalized, with the content and method of production specified at each stage. A separate index of status and applicability that can be updated independently of the controlling procedure simplifies the revision process.

Checklist

1. Conform to any existing company format.
2. Include sections covering scope, purpose, application, responsibilities, reference documents, prerequisites, and training.
3. Define how revisions are indicated in the body of the document.
4. Include a change and status page.
5. Use the future imperative tense—shall—when giving instructions.
6. Define who is responsible for updating and circulating the documents.

7. Consult widely on all interfaces.
8. Prepare an outline and agree before developing the detail.
9. Discuss and resolve all contentious issues.
10. Identify any software or hardware requirements, preparing a statement of user requirements for estimation.
11. Gain approval of the statement of user requirements.
12. Develop the full procedure.
13. Issue and circulate to all holders of any CAD/CAM procedures.
14. Train all users in the procedure.
15. Monitor the effectiveness of the procedure and revise as necessary.

9.8 Preparation of Procedures

The importance of the CAD/CAM system and its efficient operation should be made clear to all staff members within the company. This is especially true of the senior staff, which may be required to assist in the production of the new CAD/CAM procedures. The fact that the company will be following these procedures or their derivatives for a number of years and that they define, at a detailed level, the impact of CAD/CAM on the company's operation should underline their importance and the need to involve senior staff.

To ensure that the preparation of an update or a new procedure is carried out efficiently, a single person, the procedure writer, should be assigned direct responsibility for preparing the document and given a budget and work plan. A number of experienced staff members should be allocated to assist the procedure writer in this work. They will be expected to use their knowledge and experience to help the procedure writer identify the most appropriate work flow and responsibilities. It is important that full use be made of all the available CAD/CAM experience during procedure preparation. This will help to ensure that full use is made of all the system's capabilities.

Care should be taken to identify and approach the most critical topics early in the implementation. These will vary from company to company, but ensuring that, for instance, the standard data is correct from both an engineering and computer point of view will be more critical than deciding whether the print room or a system operator should be made responsible for plotter supplies.

The first step in preparing any procedure is to decide its scope and purpose and how it will interface with all existing standards and procedures. This will ensure that any impact on the company's existing working methods is both recognized and taken into account.

With innovation and the introduction of proven CAD/CAM methods, operational efficiency can be improved through procedures. This will not be the case if existing manual methods are mirrored without due recognition of the technology and its most effective utilization. To gain the most from the introduction of new methods they must be appropriate to both the installed system and the company. Identifying how existing practice can best be improved requires experience and knowledge of CAD/CAM and its likely impact on the company. The initial step should be to analyze the requirements and prepare an outline of the proposed working method. This outline should not fully develop the methodology, but define in a few key steps the proposed procedure.

Preparation and circulation of an outline ensures that the basic underlying method is understood and agreed upon before a procedure is fully developed. The outline should be circulated to all interested parties for comment and review of both the technical and procedural content. Any contentious issues should be discussed with the originating party to ensure that they are resolved through mutual agreement before their incorporation.

Once the outline has been agreed upon, the writer should analyze all the steps in detail, using the information obtained during review of the outline. No major new activities should be specified at this stage, but the identified steps should be fully detailed.

Any specific additional software, hardware, or training needs should be identified and prepared as a formal statement of user requirements. The statement should not contain reference to system commands or specific hardware, except as examples, but should fully and clearly specify the required capability. This will allow the company to establish the resources and time required to provide any additional facilities and enable management to review the costs of implementing the procedure.

9.9 Implementation of Procedures

Once the CAD/CAM procedure has been approved and adopted by the company, it should be circulated to all necessary parties and the corresponding training should be arranged for. Rather than giving a copy to all system users, it may be more effective to have a copy available by each terminal. Other copies should be available for general reference away from the system. The procedure circulation list should be controlled and reviewed each time any procedure or update is circulated.

Procedure training should be carried out by the responsible manager or supervisor. It should consist of a brief presentation of the scope and purpose of each procedure and should outline working methods. It should highlight interfaces and key points. The training should stress that procedures are live documents that will be revised in the light of experience. All users should be encouraged to provide comment and feedback to refine the procedures and improve their content.

The initial creation of CAD/CAM procedures will require a significant contribution from the CAD/CAM manager. Their maintenance and consolidation can, however, in most circumstances, be delegated to another member of the CAD/CAM team. This person should have a good knowledge of the procedures and be made responsible for their update and control as instructed by the CAD/CAM manager.

As part of the overall company quality-control system, the CAD/CAM procedures should have their effectiveness reviewed by management at regular intervals. The objective of the review is to ensure that the procedures are being adhered to and that their scope, purpose, and content are still appropriate.

9.10 Conclusion

Procedures must be recognized as a means to an end and not an end in themselves. Procedures are time-consuming to prepare and maintain, but they are vital to the long-term success of any CAD/CAM installation. Since their development requires input from all levels, CAD/CAM procedure preparation can provide a way for all staff members to contribute toward change in the working environment.

Chapter

10

Training for CAD/CAM

Training is carried out to help people in the company (be they drafters, CEOs, or whoever) understand how to carry out their jobs as effectively as possible in the new environment that results from the decision of top management to apply CAD/CAM techniques. The environment will not change abruptly. It will change over a long period. Consequently, training will not be an on-off activity, but a continuing one.

Training is of particular interest to the CAD/CAM manager because the results of using the system (and consequently the future of the CAD/CAM manager) are closely related to the quality and quantity of training. It is the responsibility of the CAD/CAM manager to define how much training people need and to ensure that such training is available and given. Owing to the importance of training, the CAD/CAM manager will want to implement procedures to check that the training is having the desired effect.

10.1 The Importance of Training

Without adequate training the benefits envisaged from the implementation of the system may never be fully realized and only very localized benefits will accrue. All CAD/CAM installations look for improved productivity and efficiency far beyond that achieved with the conventional manual methods. Without the proper training these benefits will be unobtainable, and the statement that it is more efficient to continue using the drawing board will regrettably be true.

In any proposal for a project involving capital expenditure on computer-based equipment, the first item to be reduced in value or totally removed is often the training budget. This is particularly true with CAD/CAM projects because management usually feels that a lot of risk is already being taken by spending a considerable amount of money on complex and powerful hardware and software and that there is little point in increasing the risk by spending even more money, particularly on something as intangible as training. However, this reasoning is completely erroneous because the investment in training actually reduces the risk associated with the total investment.

To reduce the possibility of the training budget being cut, the CAD/CAM manager should both educate management to understand why training is so necessary and do everything possible to fix the training item in the overall CAD/CAM project budget. When the budget is first being discussed, the CAD/CAM manager should inform everyone involved that if training is not included, it would be better to abandon the project. Before starting the project it must be understood and agreed that training is expensive, is necessary, and continues long after initial system installation. The CAD/CAM manager should produce a detailed plan showing the type and amount of training needed for each person. This plan, and its cost, need to be fully and openly discussed and agreed to. Once management is publicly committed to this plan, the risk of the training item disappearing from the budget is significantly reduced.

High technology almost inevitably carries with it a need for high levels of training. Some companies have realized this. Many of the leading high-technology companies throughout the world spend 3 to 4 percent of sales turnover for training. The great majority of companies, though, are very backward in their attitude and commitment to training. Their expenditures for training barely rise to a few tenths of 1 percent. It is hardly surprising that such companies find it hard to compete and—despite high levels of capital expenditure and an impressive panoply of high technology—show few signs of achieving the potential benefits.

10.2 Types of Training

There are five different types of training which are required for successful implementation of CAD/CAM (Table 10.1): awareness training, basic user training, advanced-application user training, manager and supervisor training, and CAD/CAM system management training. They are described in detail in Sections 10.5 to 10.9.

Many people within the company need to be trained. The first group that comes to mind is the direct users of CAD/CAM. There will be drafters and designers working in different areas such as mechanical engineering, electronic engineering, hydraulic and electrical circuit design, NC part programming, sheet metal development, and piping layout.

TABLE 10.1 The Five Types of CAD/CAM Training

Training type	Main classes of recipients
Awareness training	Everybody concerned by CAD/CAM (inside and outside engineering)
Basic user training	Users
Advanced-application user training	Users
Manager and supervisor training	All managers and supervisors concerned with CAD/CAM (inside and outside engineering)
CAD/CAM system management training	CAD/CAM manager CAD/CAM team

The managers and supervisors of direct users will also need to be trained, as will those indirect users in areas such as purchasing and marketing, who make use of information generated on the CAD/CAM system. Those directly involved in supporting use of the CAD/CAM system, such as the CAD/CAM manager, the CAD/CAM team programmers, and database specialists, will need to be educated. This group may also include company personnel who are selected to give CAD/CAM training and "superusers" who have a very good understanding of the system and can assist their colleagues.

There is another very important group of people that needs to be trained—top management. Without their understanding, commitment, and support it is unlikely that the implementation of CAD/CAM will be successful. Then there are all those in the company who appear to have no connection at all with CAD/CAM. It might be thought that there is no reason to train such people. On the other hand, there is little to lose by giving them a minimum of training, and everything to gain from the viewpoints of company image, company culture, and a better understanding of the company.

While some of these groups of people may only receive one type of training, others will receive, at different times, several types. As the company applies CAD/CAM to more application areas, such as structural analysis and NC programming, so the number and variety of courses will increase.

It should not be forgotten that many of the people that are to be trained have not learned new skills for a long time and may find it hard to assimilate information. There will also be those who were not trained properly in the first place and experience problems even when working in the traditional environment. Allowance should be made for this. Training is not a theoretical exercise carried out with perfect students having identical and complete knowledge, experience, and skills. It is a very practical exercise involving real people in the real world. Even though there will be those who want to reduce training to the very minimum, it is best to train as many people as possible as broadly as possible. Although some of the training may be wasted, the overall effect on the understanding of CAD/CAM and on morale will be positive.

10.3 Timing of Training

The CAD/CAM manager will eventually convince people of the need for training but will generally find that the dates proposed for training are not suitable. In fact, it will soon become apparent that it is never the right time for training. Users are always far too busy working on projects, and managers already have far too many things to do. Although people agree that training is necessary, they cannot find the time for it. In some cases, of course, the inability to find the time will result from hostility toward CAD/CAM or a lack of interest in it. Whatever the reason, though, the CAD/CAM manager should be aware that this problem will arise and should plan well in advance to overcome it.

At the very earliest stages of the company's involvement with CAD/CAM, before a CAD/CAM system or even a CAD/CAM manager has been selected, training is clearly required. At this time, the company knows little about CAD/CAM and needs to learn a lot before making decisions that are of strategic importance. The sooner the education process begins, the sooner the company can make productive use of CAD/CAM. The best person to train first is probably the candidate CAD/CAM manager, or (if this is not the same person) the person who will be responsible for developing the CAD/CAM strategy. Both at the earliest stages and later on, the first people to train are those who need the training most urgently and those who, as a result of the training, will be able to show successful results quickly. Throughout the CAD/CAM implementation process it will be found that visible success is the best inducement to further progress.

In the same way that those who are to be involved in developing the CAD/CAM strategy and selecting a CAD/CAM solution should be trained before the investment starts, potential users of the system should be trained before the system is installed. This will mean that once the system arrives it can be used immediately for at least some project work, with consequent positive psychological results.

By the time that the training course has been completed, follow-up actions and procedures should be in place. This subject is discussed in more detail in Section 10.10. It is an important point, since in some cases companies have done everything possible to provide the best possible training, only to find that after training, people were frustrated and demotivated by the impossibility of actually putting their new skills into practice.

The difficulty of finding the "right" time for training was mentioned above. The easiest way to get around this is to establish a direct link between training and increased productivity. This will help overcome management's reluctance and will also be good for trainees' morale. An alternative is to carry out training during periods when the workload is low, although this clearly has disadvantages since it may not be possible to match these periods, if any, to training requirements. Another alternative is to carry out training outside normal working hours, for example, in the evening. This should be acceptable for management training, although it may not appeal to all users. Instead of carrying out all the training outside company hours, it may be more suitable to carry out a part during company hours and a part outside of company hours.

To close this section on the timing of training, it is worth repeating that training is a continuous activity that does not start after system installation and stop a few days later. It will continue as long as CAD/CAM is in use. People who have not been trained, such as new staff and those not previously affected by CAD/CAM, need to receive basic training. People who have already been trained need to learn more so that they can further improve the effectiveness of their use of CAD/CAM.

It cannot be overemphasized that training is a continuous process and does not stop after the system is implemented. Awareness training should be repeated every year, with the course contents being updated to take into account the latest status of the CAD/CAM system and the company's future plans. User and systems training should take place each time there is an upgrade of the hardware or software. This need not necessarily be a full course but could be in the form of an issue of a bulletin giving the latest information and describing how it will affect the users.

Application training is a continuous process of improvement and learning from experience. It is here that user groups play a vital role in ensuring that the most effective methods are used and documented for the benefit of all. Should the company move into a new business area, then the appropriate applications training should be given. Management training should be provided whenever the company changes its procedures and working practices significantly, in order that the CAD/CAM system can be managed to best suit the new requirements. A management refresher course should be given yearly.

10.4 Sources of Training

There is a wide range of sources of CAD/CAM training. Some of them focus on providing a particular type of training at a particular time in the CAD/CAM implementation process. There are some that provide services to individuals, others that serve small or large groups.

It is convenient to split the sources into those that are internal to the company and those that are external to it. The internal sources include the CAD/CAM team (selected company staff given the role of "trainer") and friendly colleagues. Normally, internal sources will provide services on-site. Among the external sources are consultants, the CAD/CAM system vendor, CAD/CAM training companies, CAD/CAM training package vendors, and educational institutions offering CAD/CAM courses. Some of these sources, such as consultants and CAD/CAM vendors, may be prepared to offer their services on either their own premises or the company's.

The extent to which different sources are used will depend on a variety of factors such as the amount and type of training included in the system purchase contract, the total amount of money available for training, the availability of people and equipment for training activities, and the company's overall training policy.

There are advantages and disadvantages associated with each source of training. For example, educational institutions often provide a relatively low-cost service, but the quality of the service can range from poor to excellent. Internal training, developed by the company's own personnel, will often be well tuned to company requirements. This is rarely the case with external sources. The CAD/CAM system vendor usually gives good system management training; the same is often true of their basic user training. Sometimes the vendor will also have industry-experienced, applications-oriented trainers who can give very good advanced-application user training.

The CAD/CAM vendor may prefer to give courses at its own site, arguing that students will benefit from being free of everyday distractions. The company may prefer to see these courses given on its own site, with the training oriented to the work encountered on real projects and carried out in the real environment, helping to make possible the easy identification and correction of any problems that occur.

The company may decide to build up its own training force. This method can be effective because these trainers will understand the company's needs, speak the language of their colleagues, and can develop the training to meet specific requirements. If the trainers only have a part-time training role and continue part-time with their previous responsibilities, they will not run the risk of their skills and knowledge being overtaken by those of their students. On the other hand, the company may not have sufficient resources to invest in its own internal training force (even if it is only part time). An added problem is that the people selected to be trainers may not have really mastered the subject themselves, or, for some other reason, are not effective trainers. The CAD/CAM manager will need to select the most suitable sources of training and periodically check the quality of the training given.

The primary sources of training for the various categories discussed above are shown in Table 10.2. User and systems training are usually best provided by the vendors or an approved third party such as a university or technical institute. Application training is specific to a particular business and can be developed in-house in conjunction with the vendor. Awareness and management training are not provided by the CAD/CAM vendors (although they do play an educational role during the strategy evaluation and selection process). This type of training is best provided by consultants in conjunction with the CAD/CAM team. Consultants often have a background of user and system management and broad experience in CAD/CAM use and management across a range of industries.

The open-learning concept can be applied to CAD/CAM training. It allows the trainee the opportunity to learn wherever, whenever, and at whatever pace is suitable. It uses video- and audiotape media, as well as written material in the form of notes and exercises. This means that the trainee can study in the car or on the train while traveling to and from work, and at home as well as at work. It encourages the concept of training partly on company time and partly in the trainee's own time.

10.5 Awareness Training

This type of training should be given at some time to the entire staff, though the level and quantity may vary. The implementation of a

TABLE 10.2 Some Sources of CAD/CAM Training and Education

Sources	Strong points	Type of training
Internal Sources		
CAD/CAM team	Good understanding of the way that the system is used in the company	Awareness, user
Super-users		User
Internal trainers		User, supervisor
External Sources		
System vendor	Good understanding of system	User, system
CAD/CAM training company	Knowledge of training techniques and system	User
CAD/CAM training package vendor	Oriented to a particular system. Training at user's own pace.	User
Educational institutions	Low cost	User
Consultants	Good at educating management	Awareness, management

CAD/CAM system is likely to affect the working methods of many people in the company, not just those who will use the system. It will certainly change the way the company operates—its procedures and practices—and it is therefore vital that everyone should understand the CAD/CAM context. Part of this understanding process is aimed at removing fears that people may have for their jobs or their function within the organization. It is critical to the success of a CAD/CAM implementation that it have the support of the staff. Companies which undertake awareness training often do so some months after the system has been installed, but this is like shutting the stable door after the horse has gone.

The first group of people in the company that needs to be made aware of CAD/CAM is top management; until they have some understanding of CAD/CAM and are prepared to offer it some support, little progress can be made. It will be useful for them to learn about the way in which CAD/CAM can be used in a company, the way in which other companies have used it, and the potential costs and benefits.

Many companies misguidedly undertake the system selection process on their own and without recourse to the wealth of experience accumulated over the last 20 years. They allow strategy development and system selection to be undertaken by a keen engineer and/or someone nominated by the data processing department. Neither of these individuals will have any knowledge of CAD/CAM systems except for reading the odd journal article and looking at all the tempting ads. And yet these can be the very people tasked with moving the company technologically into the next decade. The very first thing they must do is to obtain some awareness training.

Awareness training can be obtained from a variety of sources, including

1. Journals and magazines
2. Exhibitions
3. Conferences and seminars
4. CAD/CAM vendors
5. Courses
6. Consultants
7. "Open learning"
8. Awareness programs of seminars, literature, and videos sponsored by industry associations, government departments, and educational institutions

Once those spearheading the selection process have a good understanding of CAD/CAM, the next people requiring a similar level of understanding are those managers and key users who are going to be closely involved with the selection process. These are the people who will have to agree on the benefits and justification, who will assist in defining user requirements, and who will be responsible for making the system a success.

Having defined the requirements—and evaluated the most suitable systems—the next step is to gain approval for capital expenditure. This is very often a stumbling block, for after spending much time getting to the point of proposal presentation, the whole project falls on stony ground. One of the main reasons for this is that the people who must sign off on the proposal do not understand the scope and possibilities of CAD/CAM. They do not understand it technically, but, more important, they do not appreciate the impact it can and should have on the organization in terms of a new way of doing business and new ways of working.

A further critical factor in the success of a CAD/CAM installation is the support of senior management, because success is not instantaneous and the benefits may not be seen for 1 or 2 years. During this period it is vital that senior management keeps faith with the project. These issues must be understood and their implications realized before the proposal is submitted for approval. It is the responsibility of the selection team and user management to ensure that top management receives the right training. This also implies that they must appreciate the issues themselves.

Once a system has been selected and installed, it may be useful to occasionally assign one workstation to awareness training for those not actively using the system. This will help these people understand a little about CAD/CAM and help reduce whatever fears or frustrations may have been induced by the arrival of this new technology.

10.6 Basic User Training

Basic user training is the initial course during which a system user, such as a drafter, first comes into contact with the system. The course will probably include a mixture of classroom and hands-on approaches. Typically, these courses will last from 1 day for a simple two-dimensional drafting system to 5 days for a three-dimensional design system. Clearly no one comes away from such a course as an expert in using the system, but generally a sufficient grounding in system use is attained. In some cases, a few more days of training may be given a few weeks later to improve the user's ability with the system. Basic user courses are given by the system vendor, by an educational institution licensed by the vendor, or by the company's internal training team. It should be realized that such courses do not teach the user how best to use the system in a particular company environment, and that after such a course, many users will not be particularly efficient when using the system.

A typical course given by the vendor might include an overview of the system, some details on operating the system, an introduction to basic commands and functions, some information on designing in two and three dimensions and on dimensioning a part drawing, generation of a few plots, details of data and drawing management procedures, and an introduction to macro and menu development. Within the company, some further basic training may be given. This could cover company standards and procedures for using the system.

Before sending people to such courses, some companies put their potential users through simple training courses to get them used to computers, keyboards, and tablets. Some people find such acclimatization courses helpful, because they get used to tasks such as keyboard entry in a low-stress environment. It is much more cost-effective to learn how to use a keyboard in this type of course than during a 5-day vendor course packed with other, more important information.

Generally, only a small group of users will follow such a course at a particular time since it is important that the trainer be able to pay attention to each individual user's needs. Similarly, it is important that each user have reasonable access to a screen. Ideally, there should be one screen per trainee. Courses of this type are very practical; much of the potential benefit will be lost if it is not possible to have maximum hands-on access. Similarly, it is essential that the user be able to put the newly gained knowledge into practice as soon as possible after the end of the course.

The question is always asked: Who should be trained first? The first people to train are those who will use the system successfully and will not give up when the inevitable problems are met.

Another question is: How many users should be trained? Initially it is only useful to train people who are going to make serious use of the system. Since it is difficult for more than an average of three people to use one screen effectively on a single-shift basis, a rough estimate can be made of the number of people who should be trained initially.

10.7 Advanced-Application User Training

This type of training will be given as a series of courses matching the steadily progressing ability of the user. The first course will be given a few months after the basic user course, by which time the user should be familiar with the system and most of its basic functions. With all systems it will be found that there are many more possibilities available than are seen during initial training. This type of training helps the user to discover these possibilities and teaches the most effective way to apply the functions of the system to particular application areas such as part programming or kinematic analysis. Another topic covered could be the transfer of data to other systems.

Advanced-application user training will be given under somewhat similar circumstances to basic user training, although the size of the group may be smaller. The course length will usually be 3 to 5 days. Trainers giving these courses should try to identify common errors of practice among the trainees and use this information to improve the basic user course. Apart from the formal advanced-application user course, the CAD/CAM manager should promote other activities to improve users' abilities. For example, user meetings should be held regularly so that users can learn the results of different approaches to system use and exchange experience gained with particular system functions.

10.8 Manager and Supervisor Training

Since managers are invariably "busy" during the working day, it may be most suitable to train them outside of normal working hours, for example, a series of a half-dozen 2- to 3-hour evening sessions. In addition, reading matter can be provided for the managers to peruse on the weekend.

The course may be divided into two parts: a common core that is followed by all managers, and then specific sessions that are of particular interest to managers from different parts of the company. The common core would aim to inform managers of the overall objectives and capabilities of CAD/CAM, discuss management issues in the mixed manual and CAD/CAM environment, and provide some practical experience. The specific sessions would be tailored to fit the requirements of, for example, a drafting department supervisor, an EDP manager, a manager from finance, and a manager from personnel. All of these people would be interested in the common core of the course. However, there are specific topics that would be of interest to each one of them but not to the others.

The need for manager and supervisor training is very rarely appreciated when the system is implemented and is almost never budgeted for in the CAD/CAM proposal. Yet it is the supervisors and managers who are responsible for ensuring that the perceived benefits are realized. This training addresses managing in a CAD/CAM environment. It involves understanding issues such as controlling a mixed CAD/CAM and manual environment, deciding what work should be done using CAD/CAM and what should be done manually, and ensuring that work is organized and carried out according to procedures. This course will typically be of a 1- or 2-day duration and should include some practical exercises on project management and resource planning. The course must also include "hands-on" training so that managers and supervisors can operate the system to the level where they can examine drawings and models and interrogate the database. This then gives them the same managing capabilities as they had when all work was done using a drawing board. There is a school of thought that all managers and senior managers, including the CEO, should know the basics of operating the CAD/CAM system. This can certainly be a very useful vehicle to help management and staff to appreciate and understand each other's point of view.

10.9 CAD/CAM System Management Training

In many CAD/CAM installations the responsibility for management of the system rests with the engineering staff (and not with the EDP department). Whoever has the job of taking back-up copies of the data, managing the use of passwords, starting and stopping the system, and ensuring that maintenance is carried out regularly must have the appropriate training. This training is invariably provided by the system vendors and is often included in the purchase price. Courses are usually 3 to 5 days long. This training should take place at the time of system installation.

The CAD/CAM manager and all members of the CAD/CAM support team should have detailed knowledge of the system and know how to operate it and how to carry out application tasks with it. Otherwise they will not be able to provide suitable service to the users. Some of them will need to have in-depth knowledge of the system, particularly if it is relatively complex and modifications or interfaces are to be made.

Much of the required system management knowledge will not come from the formal course, but from individual learning, often acquired online while solving problems with the system. The CAD/CAM manager may decide to hold informal meetings at which system management experience can be shared.

10.10 Putting Training into Practice

Experience shows that, particularly early on when the overall level of system knowledge is low, it is very difficult for users to apply their newly found skills to everyday work. Unless suitable work is available, they will rapidly forget what they learned. Even if suitable work is available, they will quickly find themselves unable to solve relatively simple problems that were outside the scope of the training course.

There is a need for transition phases between training and unsupported everyday use of the system (Figure 10.1). The progression starts with a theoretical introduction to system use, followed by hands-on training. Then the user must be able to practice with examples that are drawn from typical use, but are not part of the current workload. During this period, support should be available on call. Similarly, in the next phase, that of starting to work on "real" tasks, support needs to be at hand. If a problem arises, the user needs to be able to find assistance rapidly. Otherwise time will be lost, mistakes will be made, and despondency will set in.

The CAD/CAM manager needs to develop plans so that at the end of the training period CAD/CAM resources and suitable work are available for the trainees. In some cases this may imply that a workstation be scheduled (either full time or part time) specifically for this activity.

The speed with which knowledge gained during training can be forgotten has implications for the number of users to be trained. There is little point in training vast numbers of users if they will not be able to put their training into practice.

10.11 The Cost of Training

When considering the cost of training, it should not be forgotten that there may also be a cost arising from not carrying out training. Awareness training may cost very little except for the price of some journals, videos, and seminar fees, but the cost in terms of time lost by not giving it may be considerable. In the absence of prior training, it is not difficult to spend between 2 and 5 work-years of effort carrying out

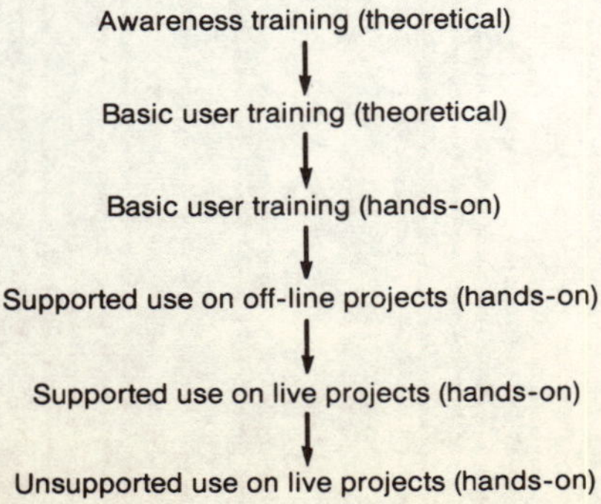

Figure 10.1 From training to practice.

system evaluation and selection. Much of this time is probably spent trying to understand the basics of CAD/CAM.

Training costs contain a component directly related to the cost of training and a component due to the loss of production during training time. The costs may appear high since between 10 and 25 days training per year per user may be required and some of the trainers may charge $5000 per week. Because the amount of training will depend on the complexity of the system and the cost of the trainer will depend on the contents of the course, it is not possible to give an average value for the cost of training. Clearly, the CAD/CAM manager will need to identify and quantify the training required in a particular company.

There is always the temptation to reduce the cost of training by cutting the training budget. However, this is counterproductive as only well-trained people will be able to deliver the promised increases in productivity. Nonetheless, there are some ways to reduce training costs without adversely affecting productivity. Some of the training may be carried out outside of normal working hours. Cheap personal computers may replace expensive workstations for some training. Sometimes it will be possible to match training with productive system use.

In many cases it will be found that the cost of training over several years will exceed the cost of the CAD/CAM system. Many CAD/CAM managers invest years of effort in selecting a CAD/CAM system. Few invest such effort in defining training requirements and selecting training solutions, although it is clear that these are also very necessary actions.

Chapter

11

Managing the Mature CAD/CAM Installation

After 12 to 18 months, depending on the size and complexity of the system, a CAD/CAM implementation will tend to mature. The CAD/CAM manager and the support team will have become experienced in the operation of the system and in dealing with the management problems which beset CAD/CAM in general. Users of the system will have mastered its commands and be capable of producing better results with CAD/CAM than with manual methods. There will be a good working relationship with the vendor, and top management should at last be aware of what the CAD/CAM system can realistically be expected to do. The short-term goals for the system will be clear, coordinated, and relate to what can actually be achieved. There are few surprises, and life, though still busy, is comfortable. It seems as if the CAD/CAM manager's role is no longer entrepreneurial, and in the future will be limited to managing the day-to-day operations of the system.

11.1 Two Views of Maturity

Top management's view of maturity will be different from that of the CAD/CAM manager. For the CAD/CAM manager, after selection of the CAD/CAM system, the first phase of the implementation is that in which the CAD/CAM manager, the support team, and the users learn how to use the system and adapt to it. The actual problems that occur are almost always unexpected, and the CAD/CAM manager's time is divided between fire fighting and trying hard to gain more knowledge of this new technique. The implementation appears to be mature when the CAD/CAM manager and the support team gain that knowledge and experience. It is likely that the CAD/CAM manager will be happy with performance at this stage. The fire fighting has died down, and for the first time it is possible to plan. Expectations have become more realistic, and the CAD/CAM manager is able to meet them.

The original implementation goals, either explicit or implicit, will have been tackled by the implementation team. Some will have been achieved, some will have been found to be too ambitious; expectations will have been lowered, and some goals will have been shelved because of a lack of resources or time. Little by little, and unnoticed by all, the implementation goals will thus have been modified, stabilized, and rationalized, and the implementation will appear to be mature.

However, the current set of ideas and objectives will have resulted from a pragmatic rationalization process unrelated to top management's requirements. Because the objectives set at the start of the project have apparently proved to be unachievable, the CAD/CAM manager will believe that the current set is what was really required. The CAD/CAM manager will believe that it is not possible to do better. Before, sights were set higher, but things didn't work out. Things now appear to be well directed; however, the fact is that the last time the plans now being followed were reviewed coldly and dispassionately was more than 12 months ago.

From the strategic level, there is another definition of maturity. It is based on the plans and objectives by which CAD/CAM is driven. From the point of view of top management, maturity means that the CAD/CAM installation has passed through the planned implementation phase and met its objectives. In practice, there may be a considerable difference between the two points of view.

11.2 Consequences of Maturity

In the same way that the CAD/CAM manager may have a false impression of the success of the implementation, there may be several other characteristics of maturity which may be misunderstood. There will be more time available for the support and development of the system, although this may only be apparent to the CAD/CAM team as an impression that they are not quite so exhausted. There is a temptation to take advantage of this by launching some improvement or integration tasks.

Far more information is kept in people's heads than is realized, but there is a limit to the amount of information that can be maintained in this way. This will become apparent when some of the key CAD/CAM staff members leave or are promoted.

Although the people concerned may not be aware of it, impetus will have been lost. Those who championed and carried out the implementation will be drained. How would they react if they were told they had to start the same implementation again from scratch? They will have paced themselves to perform a major task, they will have completed that task, and, although the work still stretches out before them undiminished, there will be a temptation to relax to a slower pace of work.

Most important of all, top managers will no longer be taking a direct interest in the progress and success of CAD/CAM implementation. After trying to be involved and give guidance in the early stages and finding the problems outside their understanding, they will have withdrawn. The CAD/CAM manager will thus have been managing the system unaided from above, led by the single broad-brush management instruction to "make the system productive."

In a traditional organization, by the very nature of the beast, the CAD/CAM manager will not have been able to apply a strategic or businesswide involvement to CAD/CAM direction. It is vital that business control of the CAD/CAM system now be reasserted.

11.3 Change of Emphasis

A different style and emphasis is required as the implementation begins to mature, and the CAD/CAM manager must be aware of the changing situation to be able to react accordingly and take advantage of new opportunities for progress. Instead of the highly pressurized and reactive situation of a brand new installation, the CAD/CAM manager will gradually find that problems become more regular, predictable, and almost repetitive. The frustration changes from a lack of experience and ability to make the barely understood happen to a lack of time and resource to make the obvious happen. The successful CAD/CAM manager will respond to this new environment by initiating four parallel and overlapping activities.

While being sensitive to the information and skills that are currently in the heads of the CAD/CAM support team and the users and being mindful of the fact that CAD/CAM experience is hard won but all too easily lost, the CAD/CAM manager will set out to define, proceduralize, consolidate, and document the working methods, system management procedures, and in-house refinements of the system.

The CAD/CAM manager should set the implementation back on its best footing and bring it back within the scope of both the engineering department and company strategy by carrying out a review which will reset the CAD/CAM project plans for the future. The impetus and opportunity to expand into new areas of development, both the development of the CAD/CAM system itself and integration with other systems and departments, will be satisfied by well-managed and well-coordinated project planning that is based on the review.

Finally, the system needs to be prepared for the future, in the knowledge that CAD/CAM, although part of the company for only a few months, will be a part of it for the coming decades and so must be run within long-term guidelines.

11.4 Consolidation

By the time that a mature, stable state is approached, the CAD/CAM team, the users, and those departments which have so far interfaced with CAD/CAM will all have become used to a certain way of working on the project. In practice, this means that they will have become used to a certain level of improvisation and "getting by." Events move so fast during the initial phases of installation and implementation that there is never enough time to absorb and record properly what is going on. Apart from the vendor's training documentation, users and CAD/CAM support staff alike will be working with their own individual notes and jottings instead of with uniform sets of thorough instructions and procedures.

A wide range of people, from users to the CAD/CAM support team and other engineering managers, will have become quite adept at working in this manner and may see it as quite natural. As the prospects arise for new initiatives for CAD/CAM, their feasibility will be evaluated in the light of this artificially low and streamlined overhead. As a result, such projects may seem very attractive.

However, time should first be set aside to restore the level of CAD/CAM training, documentation, and project control to that used on non-CAD/CAM projects. Otherwise the entire CAD/CAM project will probably suffer. A conscious effort on the part of the CAD/CAM manager will be required in order to take this step. New developments will have to wait until the current situation is properly under control.

A CAD/CAM installation will tend to decay unless it is actively managed. The most obvious and persistent cause of this decay is the dilution of skills that occurs as new users are trained and more experienced users move away. A more important component, however, is that those in charge of the remaining drawing board resource will tend to pull users away from CAD/CAM. It always seems to be "quicker" to start that rush job on the drawing board, and once the first revision has been produced, it appears that it would be a waste of effort to input the information with CAD/CAM. In this way, whole design projects may slip away from CAD/CAM to manual methods.

Users themselves will be tempted to take shortcuts at some time or other, and the CAD/CAM manager will be surprised at the number of ruses that apparently responsible drafters and designers feel are acceptable in the cause of "getting the work done." Other users may either simply not be methodical or regard taking notes to assist them to develop their CAD/CAM skills as a diversion of effort from the apparently more important task of designing.

It can be seen that even though maturity appears to have been attained, the original objectives have not really been met, and the CAD/CAM manager cannot be content merely to work on system enhancements while the users get on with the task of designing. The CAD/CAM manager and the support team must always be involved with the way the system is being used, and they must pay attention to the wider influences upon it. This involvement must continue throughout the life of the system, with similar motivation being instilled in any successor to the CAD/CAM manager.

A specific consolidation activity is necessary to freeze the current good practices and skills and make them part of the fabric of the implementation. Quality should be built into the actual running of the system, rather than being tacked on as an extra or being imposed by the watchfulness of a particular individual. Dealing with library parts or other standard information, removing the risk of duplicating graphic information on CAD/CAM and on hard copy, eliminating errors caused by in-house routines or system failure—all of these must be designed into methods of working.

11.5 Documentation

The single most important weapon in the fight against system decay is documentation. This will take the form of procedures (for both operation and use of the system), training information, operating instructions, and documentation of in-house additions or modifications to software.

The type and detail of the documentation will depend on the size of the CAD/CAM system, the size of the company itself, and the purpose to be fulfilled. In general, the larger the installation, the greater the amount of documentation, and the larger the company, the more formal the documentation will be. Large companies tend to have standard formats for documentation, including such things as drafting department manuals, and the CAD/CAM manager must create procedures and records accordingly. Small companies, on the other hand, often rely more on face-to-face agreement, and an overly complex set of instructions is likely to remain unread.

Whatever the style, the CAD/CAM manager should start creating the required documentation at the earliest opportunity and should issue it in draft form at regular intervals. This allows comment from the users, puts them on the right working lines from the start, and means that the documentation evolves smoothly instead of building up into a large task that will never be addressed. The practice of releasing draft documentation which will evolve to become the final version can help instill better documentation habits into members of the CAD/CAM support team and the users themselves.

It should be clear to the support team that it is necessary to follow good system software development practices. The users can be shown that if they keep records of the files they create and the structure of the information within those files, it will be of use to them when they meet problems or require assistance.

Although documentation is the cornerstone of consolidation, the principle of consolidation must be carried over into the consideration of how the implementation should be developed. New areas such as linking with other systems, giving information to contractors, generation of further in-house software, and indeed accepting new revisions of software from the vendor should all be considered against the strengths and weaknesses of the current implementation and should take into account the extra work involved. Starting new projects before existing ones are on a firm footing leads to short-term gains in time, but often results in loss of time and rework over the long term.

Until the CAD/CAM manager, the support team, and the users have settled into a properly controlled and organized way of working, the resource that will be required for new projects will always be underestimated and a spiral of late projects set up. If the weaknesses in the current setup are not attended to, then problems will occur "unexpectedly" in the future.

A final point about consolidation which should not be forgotten is that the vendor should be a major influence on the success and development of any CAD/CAM system. The vendor can provide support and advice on current problems, provide upgrades and new releases of software, and should be only too pleased to participate in the success of the implementation. Constructive communication and sharing of ideas between the CAD/CAM manager and the vendor is a feature of most successful implementations.

11.6 Time to Review

Once the implementation appears to have matured (some 12 to 18 months after the system was installed), it is time to look back at the original goals and requirements of CAD/CAM and assess how the current CAD/CAM implementation measures up against them. It is now time to review the CAD/CAM system, its performance within the engineering department, and its integration with other systems and departments. The CAD/CAM learning curve has been climbed, and the experience gained must be used to ensure that future work is run on the best possible lines. Objectives must be reset, effort redirected, and new projects allowed for.

11.7 Planning for the Review

An implementation review is a significant task in itself. A large number of people will have to be involved, and the CAD/CAM manager will have a great deal of collating, writing, and project planning to do. It follows that the task should be properly planned, with a sufficient amount of time allocated to it, and should be carried out with full involvement of those involved.

The framework of the review should be carefully considered and documented and the entire exercise should be recorded, in the knowledge that it will be repeated in a year and once a year every year thereafter. The CAD/CAM implementation will evolve over many years, so it is logical to review and audit the implementation regularly in order to be sure that progress and direction are optimized. Even without any growth in the power and scope of the CAD/CAM system, the review is still necessary to react to the effects of time. The system may be static, but its users, managers, and interfaces with the company are dynamic, and the company itself is in a changing environment.

11.8 The Reviewer

There are three basic principles to be followed in an implementation review: look wide, look up, and be honest. The basic choice of reviewer is between the CAD/CAM manager or an external CAD/CAM specialist. Some CAD/CAM managers can successfully carry out such a review, others cannot. If the review is to be successful, the person responsible for carrying it out must take an independent viewpoint and ensure that this independence is maintained throughout the whole exercise. The reviewer must be able to see the system as if for the first time, and be able to find out by questioning others how the system behaves, is used, should be used, and could be used. This may be difficult for the CAD/CAM manager.

It is important that the CAD/CAM manager feels able to apply this impartiality before going ahead with the task of leading the review. The person responsible for carrying out the review must not be afraid of making severe judgments about the history of the system. The CAD/CAM manager's own work may need to be questioned, and the conclusion may be that it could be significantly improved in the future.

The CAD/CAM manager's immediate superior may be able to assist with the maintenance of impartiality by monitoring the review, but if it is felt that the CAD/CAM manager cannot be sufficiently impartial, consideration should be given to bringing in outside assistance in order that the review actually produce the worthwhile and necessary results that are required.

Another factor which may influence the choice of reviewer is the profile of the CAD/CAM implementation within the company. Providing that the implementation has been successful, and has been seen as such within the company, then a review led by the CAD/CAM manager may be sufficient to reaffirm and redirect project control. If, however, it is felt that more could have been achieved with the system, or even that it has turned out to hold back rather than encourage progress within the company, the review should become a full audit and would be better carried out with the aid of an independent expert or consultant.

Finally, it should be remembered that one of the fundamental reasons for carrying out a review of the implementation is to reassert business control. Top managers will have lost interest in the implementation after trying to give guidance and finding the problems beyond their understanding. The CAD/CAM manager will thus have been managing the implementation alone and will have been able to apply little strategic or businesswide direction to CAD/CAM. A consultant-led review is beneficial if the strategic issues surrounding the system are of major importance, since it is much more likely to take a wide-ranging and balanced approach to the task.

11.9 Scope of the Review

The original justification for purchase of the CAD/CAM system should have been made on the basis of its effects on, and benefits for, the company as a whole. Even if some of the interfaces that were originally intended have not been built and the current use of the system is confined to a single engineering or drafting department, it will nevertheless be necessary to consider its interaction with the rest of the company in order to ensure that redefined objectives and plans are complete and well founded.

It certainly will be necessary to refer to the justification document on which approval for purchase was based, as well as to the original project plans for implementation and training. These should be assessed for their content, but should not necessarily be taken as a guide for redefined plans and objectives, since it is possible that the scope, detail, and even accuracy of these documents was less than ideal.

The review must be led by someone with suitable stature and experience, since it will take input from many sources, such as designers, the drafting department manager, lead users, and members of other departments such as preproduction, production, and possibly purchasing and marketing. It will also include appropriate involvement from top management in order that a complete picture be obtained.

11.10 Overview of Review Aims

To successfully carry out the review, the CAD/CAM manager must take on the role of an outsider, someone who is seeing the system and the implementation afresh or for the first time. The first task will be to stop looking at everyday system details, and take a long-term view.

The question of what should and could be gained from CAD/CAM must be asked anew. Leaving aside the practicalities and limitations of the system for the time being, what can be gained from using CAD/CAM within the engineering department? In what areas of the company or with what other systems would some form of information transfer be of benefit? Are there opportunities for automating graphic or textual operations that are found to be tedious? As the questions become more extensive, the less viable the replies become, but some valid suggestions may be offered to a reviewer who has an open mind.

A long hard look at the control of information is required: Is there a guarantee that all data is backed up? Will retrieval from archive or back-up allow the correct information to be called up? Can issued and standard data be accidentally accessed or illegally modified? Is management certain that drafters are not duplicating information on the board or on the screen?

Does the CAD/CAM manager have enough support? Is it of the right sort? Is the CAD/CAM manager involved in new projects, or are projects secretly laid out on the drawing board? Does the CAD/CAM manager have sufficient feedback from superiors about the wider implications of CAD/CAM, or from members of other departments who may feel that their work is adversely affected by CAD/CAM?

How is the CAD/CAM system accountable—for what and to whom? It may well be the case that accountability for CAD/CAM was relaxed when the first installation and implementation problems occurred. They must be reinstated, even if this superficially appears to limit freedom and flexibility of action.

Are there other projects which impact on CAD/CAM? Does CAD/CAM affect other projects? What is the role of CAD/CAM in CIM? Who is responsible for the progress and execution of model and drawing information? Is information produced as drawings simply because methodology has remained unchanged since drawing board days? Has the use, quality, and communication of information been improved? Have the company's overall requirements of CAD/CAM changed? What are the views of the user committee? Are operating procedures working? Are skill levels increasing? Are forward plans being developed? Is equipment obsolete? Are the right questions being asked?

11.11 Objectives of the Review

The framework of the review has to be established before the review itself commences. The CAD/CAM manager must be clear about objectives, since merely asking general questions of a random selection of people will produce no more than a conversational case study of the use of CAD/CAM within the company.

The objectives of the review are

1. To confirm or refute the assumptions made in the original justification
2. To compare the current position with both the justification and the original implementation plan
3. To examine the reasons for the deviations from the original plans, and to understand whether they were due to delays, failures, or valid changes of direction
4. To question the management, operational and usage patterns and procedures which have become established
5. To regenerate links with departments and managers that were expected to be concerned with CAD/CAM, but in practice are not
6. To reestablish strategic and business control over CAD/CAM
7. To redefine CAD/CAM objectives if necessary
8. To set the scene for new developments and enhancements
9. To ensure that consolidation is complete
10. To produce a layered set of CAD/CAM plans for the next 12 months

A word of caution about the review. There may be pressure from top management to rejustify the system in the light of experience. Not having had control of the system for up to a year, their first impulse may be to insist that they be supplied with the information that they have lacked and in the form that they require. Such an exercise is of limited value. If considered in terms of direct benefits alone, it will not take into account the indirect benefits, and if done in detail, it will focus excessive attention on the past rather than concentrating on future opportunities.

The report that results from a review of the CAD/CAM implementation is not something to be read once and then filed away. It must be the platform and the spur for the creation of a coordinated set of plans for all projects and activities which affect CAD/CAM. To be successful these plans must receive top-level support. They must be workable, and they must be real, live, maintained, followed, and respected by the people involved.

11.12 New Initiatives

One of the main results of the system review is a clear assessment of new project initiatives in terms of usefulness, urgency, and priority. It is only too easy, for example, to invest effort too early in glamorous integration projects such as a design-to-manufacturing interface, which would save work-hours on the shop floor, but which will not have the requisite quality controls in place for another 18 months.

As the CAD/CAM implementation becomes mature, some of the enhancements or developments which were envisaged at the outset may be seen as impractical in the light of the experience which has been gained. Conversely, new opportunities may appear as a result of experience.

It should be borne in mind that new developments are often seen as attractive both by the CAD/CAM support team, who would like something new and interesting to break the routine, and by senior management, who may be able to see the benefits without realizing the problems. The proposals for such developments need to be treated in the same logical way as all other project proposals in the company are treated.

Unless care is taken, new developments for a CAD/CAM system are unlikely to be subject to proper project control. Those associated with the implementation will have become used to an ad hoc method of working and will view possible new projects in the same light. CAD/CAM, CIM, and software developments are often seen (erroneously) as projects for which the justification is very difficult to quantify. As a result, developments tend to be based on "acts of faith." Unfortunately, implementation is then carried out on the same principle. In the technological world, acts of faith can almost always be equated with ignorance—for which a cure can be found.

There is a surprisingly high overhead in investigating and planning CIM developments, and for a project to bear fruit, a long preparation and planning phase is required. This means that assessment and research of new ideas and opportunities, for eventual presentation and approval, must start well in advance.

As seen in Chapter 2, coordination of the different developments requires a project structure that involves a management level high enough to see the business implications of each development and to assign a corresponding priority.

One of the major achievements of a successful review will be to redefine project schedules within the company's overall CIM program. The CAD/CAM manager needs to be a major participant and influence on the CIM program. Engineering information has a key role in CIM, and CIM is an area in which the role of the CAD/CAM manager clearly extends beyond the immediate confines of the engineering department.

While adhering to the precept that new initiatives should be planned with the benefit of all the hard-won experience, the CAD/CAM manager should keep a positive and forward-looking approach, staying on the lookout for new opportunities. There may be once-envisaged projects that were shelved during the early implementation, but which have now become viable. The software and hardware that the system vendor can supply will become ever more sophisticated and powerful. Other vendors' equipment develops new uses. Integration becomes feasible and justifiable in more and more areas. These possibilities must be evaluated from a companywide point of view so that business opportunities are not lost and the company does not fall behind in gaining the very technological advantage that led to the original purchase of the CAD/CAM system.

11.13 Long-Term CAD/CAM

During the installation phase CAD/CAM has been new and different, but it must eventually become an accepted part of the fabric of the company. The same is true of all computer systems. No company would take visitors into the drafting department to show them the drawing boards, and while it is to be hoped that there will always be something worth demonstrating on the CAD/CAM system, the days of giving demonstrations simply because the equipment is new and expensive will disappear.

Even though the system may currently only have a history of 1 or 2 years, there will come a time when the people who use it will have known no other way of working and cannot remember when there was not a CAD/CAM system in the company.

The CAD/CAM manager of a maturing system must therefore establish the framework on which CAD/CAM will be run to the year 2000 and beyond. Skill dilution, personnel rotation and development, and lack of adherence to procedures will all tend to make the implementation decay. Encouragement of CAD/CAM growth and prevention of decay will be equally important activities.

Although it may appear on the surface to be stable, a successful CAD/CAM system is in fact a growing and regenerating organism. Users become more skilled and take on new responsibilities. Some will be promoted or will have moved on to non-CAD/CAM projects, as they must be if they are not to feel trapped by their CAD/CAM role. New blood will have to be trained. It is easy to forget how long it took experienced CAD/CAM users to get up to speed and to expect new users of the system to work at the same high level. The replacement of old users by new users dilutes the CAD/CAM skill base, and unless this problem is addressed the performance of CAD/CAM will decline.

There are many influences on the development of CAD/CAM within the company. The marketing department may be so pleased with its potential for impressing customers that they take up a great deal of user time creating demonstrations for potential clients. The preproduction department may value the quality of work that they have begun to receive from the system, or conversely they may have found that a series of preproduction runs have been delayed because design information from CAD/CAM was released late. The financial department may become concerned at the size of the CAD/CAM overhead and wish to see evidence that suitable business benefits are accruing.

Such influences increase as integration projects develop, creating interfaces that open up the possibility of information flow throughout the company. These influences coupled with the internal state of flux mean that CAD/CAM can never be managed as a background activity—the manager and the support team must always be active on its behalf, because without their involvement and commitment the system will stagnate and decay. Positive action will resolve the problems that are likely to arise.

Training should help to overcome the effects of personnel rotation. Methods of pooling user-developed techniques, such as macro roundups and skills workshops, should be devised. Some inventiveness with the format will help. CAD/CAM cartoons and tongue-in-cheek dictums are more easily remembered than dry procedural documentation. Personnel development can fill skill gaps. Users and managers must not be held back simply because they are too skilled.

Resources for new projects should be allocated to build the basic enhancements that the users call for as they gain more experience. Plans for all projects should exist as a result of the review, and the review should be carried out annually to maintain this focus and ensure that system and personnel changes are accommodated.

In the long term, relationships with both the vendor and the user group can never be too strong. The vendor should be made to participate in the success of the implementation. User groups provide a forum through which knowledge of the best practice of each area of implementation can be gained.

Management of a mature CAD/CAM implementation requires that many of the virtues needed for the initial installation, such as the ability to assimilate information rapidly, the ability to work in an environment of rapid change, the ability to implement a "get by" solution now and look for the better answer later, are superseded. The mature implementation is more oriented toward consolidation, review, development of new initiatives and personnel, attention to procedure and detail, and ensuring that CAD/CAM fits properly into CIM.

It seems almost as if the initial phase of CAD/CAM installation requires a CAD/CAM manager who is a real leader and entrepreneur, whereas in the mature implementation these qualities are no longer needed. They appear to be replaced by that quality of the traditional middle manager—the ability to provide smooth running of current operations on a day-to-day basis.

11.14 The Future

Yet, that is not the end of the story. The consolidated, mature CAD/CAM installation provides the necessary, solid basis for the following phase. In this phase, which very few companies have reached today, engineering information and CAD/CAM play key strategic roles. They are the resource and the tool that will be at the heart of product innovation and quality in the future. Those companies that use them efficiently and entrepreneurially will gain a competitive advantage. In the same way that information and information technology have revolutionized industries such as airlines and banks, engineering industries will also be revolutionized. The resource (information) and the tool (CAD/CAM) are identified. Top management is faced with a critical problem—how to use them effectively.

INDEX

About the Author

John Stark, Ph.D., has been active in the field of technical computing since 1967. Dr. Stark has been involved extensively in the development and implementation of CAD/CAM systems in Europe and the United States and has served as a CAD/CAM expert for the United Nations in the Far East. Currently Dr. Stark is a director of Coopers & Lybrand Associates Europe, where he is responsible for CAD/CAM and CIM management consulting. He resides in Geneva, Switzerland.